MANDARIN GRADE 3

MANDARIN GRADE 3

JAMES HUME

The Pentland Press
Edinburgh·Cambridge·Durham

First published in 1993 by
The Pentland Press Ltd.
1 Hutton Close
South Church
Bishop Auckland
Durham

ISBN 1 85821 060 7

Typeset by Spire Origination Ltd., Norwich
Printed and bound by Antony Rowe Ltd., Chippenham,
Wiltshire SN14 6LH

To my wife

Contents

Chapter 1

Hors d'Oeuvres

It was while I was a pupil at George Heriot's School, Edinburgh, in the 1930s, that there first crossed my mind the idea that I might perhaps make my career in what was then called, with suitable deference, the Higher Civil Service.

There was no family pressure in that direction. My father, a middle-grade administrative employee in local government, had only one firm piece of advice — that I should not enter local government. Apart from taking a close interest in my progress at school and doing all he could to encourage it — no wireless programmes were allowed to interfere with my homework at the living-room table — he was content to let events take their course. Having served in the Indian Army for a time in the first war, he made occasional remarks about the attractions of the Indian Civil Service. But these were never recommendations; and it was no doubt apparent to him, as it was to me, that I was a fairly unadventurous lad, interested to read about distant lands across the sea, but not eager to contemplate the prospect of living there.

My mother, a practical woman not given to flights of fancy, was concerned only that I should get a good safe job. These, after all, were the troubled days of the 1930s, and though we as a family suffered no economic hardship, dark clouds sat on the horizon. What that good safe job might be she did not presume to say; but such a prospect for the future meant that I had to 'stick in' at school. She did, it is true, remark occasionally, 'You were born to be a gentleman.' I had no illusions about this being anything more than a comment on my tendency sometimes to spend too long with a book in an armchair when there were household tasks to be done.

Heriot's was a fee-paying grant-aided school for about 1600 boys. The fees were very modest — only £12 a year in the senior classes — which meant that

1

the pupils tended to come from lower-middle class or working class homes rather than from the wealthier professional classes. It was a no-nonsense establishment in the Scottish academic tradition and particularly strong in mathematics and science. One of my neighbours in class eventually became Professor of Pure Mathematics at Cambridge. (Unknown to me, there was another boy called Mackay a few classes below who was doing very well in mathematics. In due course he gave up a promising academic career in that subject, and trained for the Bar. He did very well at that too; he could hardly have done better, for he became Lord Chancellor.)

As I progressed up the senior school it became clear that though I was competent enough in the favoured fields of mathematics and science, I was no more than that; and I began to be bored. It was only in the sixth year when I dropped physics and chemistry and devoted more time to history and languages that I realised that my interests and talents lay in these fields — especially history, under the influence of a very lively teacher.

This focusing of intellectual interest made me decide to go to Edinburgh University and study history. I had no clear idea what I would do after that — in 1939/40 clear ideas about the future were not in many people's reckoning. I had, however, learned that down the years there had been a steady trickle of bright lads from Heriot's who had gone into the Administrative Grade of the Civil Service after having 'done', as we said, history at Edinburgh University. Their example was filed away at the back of my mind.

In these days before student grants, the annual Bursary Competition run by the University was an important event for scores of boys and girls in their final year at school. Although there were other ways of financing oneself at the university, a sufficiently high place in that competition assured an income that would meet the needs of all except the big spenders. I presented myself with a large number of other young hopefuls outside the Examination Hall in the Old Quadrangle one fine morning early in May 1940. The war, if indeed there was a war, was very far away; spring had come; and we looked forward to the last day of the exams on 10th May. When we appeared on that morning, the wireless bulletins were still ringing in our ears. German aircraft had bombed Holland and Belgium; the phoney war was over.

A few weeks later I was awarded a university bursary which, along with another from the school, would more than meet my modest needs. For the next two years I enjoyed the intellectual stimulus and the camaraderie of university life, even although studies of medieval kingship or eighteenth century politics were accompanied by fire-watching, square-bashing and bad news. In 1942 I joined the Royal Air Force. My three years there probably contributed as much to my general education and development as it did to the war effort. In October 1945, I was fortunate to be back — some of my friends were not so fortunate — in the Old Quadrangle to begin the third year of my interrupted four-year course.

How I enjoyed that blissful return! Not all the austerities of post-war Britain could dull the sense of liberation and exhilaration. I did not find it difficult to resume the discipline of study, nor was there any problem in combining my exploration of the past with a variety of extra-curricular activities. A strong interest in current affairs led me into various student societies and university debates though I was too pragmatic in my approach to adopt the general philosophy, far less become a member, of any political party.

As the months slipped pleasantly by, the question of a future career became more and more insistent. I hoped, and indeed expected, to get a first. It was conceivable that I could spend my life as an academic. A professor from my 1940–42 period, now Director of the Institute of Historical Research, V. H. Galbraith, a great character, a great scholar, and a great stimulator, with whom I was still in touch, suggested that after leaving Edinburgh I should go to Oxford. I was indeed offered a place at Balliol. But I had doubts about this. Was I entirely suited temperamentally to the academic life? Did I want to devote myself to research, teaching and writing? Going to Oxford would not, it is true, commit me one way or another; but during my stay there the basic question of future career would have to be faced as I was facing it now. Perhaps I should have set these tiresome questions aside and been more eager to launch out and sample the opportunities and the enrichment which Oxford would no doubt have offered. Rightly or wrongly I did not. I was too concerned to grasp the nettle now rather than two years later.

I thought more and more about these former pupils of Heriot's whose footsteps I had followed to the history classrooms of the university. Should I not follow them further into the world of government and administration? My years in the Old Quad and on various windswept airfields in England and Scotland had not produced any burning passion to be a civil servant. (Does anyone have a burning passion to be a civil servant? *Ought* anyone to have a burning passion to be a civil servant?) On the other hand I had developed no entrepreneurial instincts, graduates were not sought as eagerly by industry as they are now, and the possibility of school teaching never seriously entered my head. The more I surveyed the possibilities, the more I returned to thoughts of the Civil Service. I was after all very interested in public affairs and was eager in some way to promote the public good; I had some capacity for organising facts and arguments and expressing these reasonably clearly orally and in writing; I had no party political loyalties and would not therefore be likely to find myself frustrated by working towards general goals with which I fundamentally disagreed (though I was realistic enough to accept that from time to time in any organisation one might have to promote some particular course of action with which one did not agree). The Civil Service seemed a means of combining these interests and capabilities with the need to earn a living.

Before the war, the competition for entry to the Administrative Grade (i.e. the senior ranks) of the Civil Service took the form of a written examination in some group of subjects at Honours Degree level followed by an interview. This had been suspended during the war. Immediately after the war a new type of entry competition was introduced to cope with the large number of candidates, including ex-service men and women, many of whom had not been able to complete or even start their university studies while engaged on war work. This new 'Reconstruction' competition, as it was called, was open to honours graduates and any men and women who could produce evidence that they were likely or would have been likely to get at least a second-class honours degree. The competition consisted of three stages. The first was a written examination in English, arithmetic and general subjects plus intelligence tests. This was a qualifying and eliminating examination; unless a certain level of performance was achieved the candidate fell by the wayside and did not proceed any further. Stage 2 was a two-day series of tests and interviews at a country house deep in the English countryside, designed to produce a rounded picture of the candidate's qualities, abilities and personality before Stage 3. This final stage of the competition was an interview before a body known as the Final Selection Board which made the decision to accept or not to accept the candidate.

I took the written exam — in the familiar territory of Edinburgh University examination hall hired for the purpose by the Civil Service Commission — towards the end of 1946. There came a few weeks later an invitation to take part in Stage 2 at the Manor House, Stoke d'Abernon, Surrey. One snowy day in February 1947 I boarded the *Flying Scotsman*. As we sped south across the flat, white-blanketed lands of eastern England no one on that train could have known that we were only at the beginning of what was to be the worst winter of the post-war years. Grim shadowy towns drifted past, cowering beneath the snow. I saw nothing of London in the tube between King's Cross and Waterloo, but in Surrey snow was piled high on station platforms. Muffled figures stepped out into the mirk. Some with bowler hats and brief cases had no doubt spent the day in Whitehall. (Would I in ten or twenty years time be just like them? A brief-case perhaps; but a bowler hat — certainly not!) From Stoke d'Abernon station I and other guests of the Civil Service Commission were driven slowly along narrow lanes to the Manor House.

Some sections of the Press had been highly critical of the Reconstruction competition, particularly the role of the 'country house party'. Was this not a means of keeping out of the higher ranks of the Civil Service honest but able sons of toil whose manners and deportment were not those of the exclusive élite who ran the Civil Service? Instead of qualifications for entry being determined by the more or less objective test of written examination, the new system, it was suggested, would smooth the path for those with the gift of the gab, the right (i.e. public school) accent, and the right (i.e. upper middle-class Home Counties) background. I did not myself think this at all likely. Whatever might happen in some sections of society it seemed to me that the Civil Service with its long tradition of competitive examination and search for intellectual quality was unlikely to have abandoned that search — however much the new style of competition might seek other qualities as well as the purely intellectual.

The Chairman of the Board referred to those Press comments when he gave an introductory talk. No one would be marking us for table manners; if we chose to eat peas from our knives, so be it. He described what would happen in the next couple of days. The object was to build up as complete a picture as possible of the intellectual and personal qualities of each of us. This would be presented to the Final Selection Board to be used by them as background when we appeared before them for the all-important final interview.

My recollections of the next few days are stronger on impression than on detail. But I do remember an experience known as 'The Island Story'. Each of us was given a file of papers about a mythical island, its resources, its people and its problems. We met in small groups, each candidate serving in turn as chairman with certain specific problems to be discussed and action decided. Members of the Board sat in the background taking notes about each individual's performance as a chairman and as a committee member. Apart from this, there were more intelligence tests; each of us had to address a meeting; and there were several personal interviews with staff — with an 'observer' concerned primarily with intellectual qualities, a psychologist interested in character, personality and general interests, and a chairman whose responsibility it was to make an all-round assessment.

Of the problems discussed, the questions asked and the answers given, I remember nothing. But the impression remains of a relaxed and friendly atmosphere. The interviews seemed concerned not to expose deficiencies but to encourage the whole person to declare himself. When we departed for Stoke d'Abernon station I was not the only one who confessed he had quite enjoyed himself. A few weeks later I was summoned to attend the Final Selection Board in London. By now snow and ice had caused widespread disruption. Trains were late or failed to run; coal sat immobile in railway sidings; there were even more shortages than usual; and there was a ban on the use of electricity during certain parts of the day. I managed somehow to get to the Savile Row entrance of Burlington House on the right day at the right time, and was ushered into an unlit, unheated waiting room. Soon a messenger appeared bearing a lighted candle. He asked me to follow him, watching carefully where I put my feet. In near darkness I was led up a rather grand staircase, our shadows flickering on the walls. Up we went until we came to an equally grand doorway. My guide stopped outside it. Was I ready? I was as ready as I was likely to be. He knocked, opened the door, bellowed, 'Mr Hume, sir,' and propelled me inside.

Before me in a gloomy cavern was a table. On that table were seven candles and behind each candle sat a human form. Six of them were wrapped in coats and scarves; the seventh, uncoated, motioned to me to sit at the other side of the table. He introduced himself as the Chairman. I was now face to face with the Final Selection Board.

Six of my interviewers were male; one was female, a very soignée middle-aged lady. She and the Chairman had faint smiles of welcome; the others had expressions of mingled boredom and distaste. The morning was by now well-advanced; other young aspirants had appeared before them; and all except the Chairman looked cold in spite of their overcoats and mufflers. He, perhaps hardier than the rest, perhaps concerned to show the stuff of which senior civil servants are made, made do with his sober grey suit. After all, he was, as I later learned, Sir Percival Waterfield, head of the Civil Service Commission. I never learned who the others were, but I sometimes thought I would like to have known more about that attractive lady. All were, I suppose — for this is how these Boards were formed — senior people from industry, the academic world or some form of public service.

The Chairman started off in quite a kindly way and went over with me my career to date. Then he said he would invite his colleagues to ask me some questions. At this point the kindliness dried up and for the next forty minutes or so I was subjected to a very firm interrogation. I have no recollection of the questions, but as from Stoke d'Abernon I retain some very clear impressions. In contrast to Stoke d'Abernon it was almost as if the object was to show up any weaknesses. Replies were often followed by supplementary questions such as, 'What do you mean by . . .?' or 'Why do you think that . . .?' Any vagueness or evasiveness in an answer was immediately pounced on and probed thoroughly. The questioning was hard but not unfair. When it was over, the Chairman indicated that I would be informed of the result in due course. I rose and, realising for the first time that I had had a severe going over, tottered to the door.

In a few weeks, a buff envelope from the Civil Service Commission dropped through the letter-box. Inside was a request that I present myself for medical examination by a consultant physician in Glasgow. There was no comment on my performance before the Final Selection Board and no indication whether I was accepted. But at the top corner of the note there was a reference number followed by the letters SUCC. This inspired a surge of hope. Was I really successful? They would not presumably send for medical examination people who had failed.

By now the drama of the winter was over and the only problem in getting to my medical appointment was finding my way in that part of Glasgow's West End where consultants saw their private patients. My encounters with doctors had fortunately been rare and uncomplicated, but a certain apprehension had never been very far away. Perhaps I was more apprehensive than I thought that day. Halfway through the examination the doctor surprised me by asking if I felt quite well. Did I take unusually hard physical exercise? I was flummoxed by this but answered 'Yes' and 'No' respectively. He carried on with his examination and then asked me to lie down and rest for a while on a couch. He went out and left me to my thoughts. Curiously, I was more puzzled than concerned; I did not feel ill and did not seem to be dying. As I lay alone in that quiet room at the back of an elegant Glasgow terrace, a feeling of philosophic calm stole over me.

After I suppose ten or fifteen minutes the doctor returned and resumed his examination. Without saying anything specific, he seemed more cheerful about my prospects. When he had finished, he said that my blood pressure had been high but after the rest it had subsided. Again without spelling out any particulars he implied that he was satisfied. I bade him farewell and, thankful to be able to re-join the human race, I made my way through the crowds in Sauchiehall Street to Queen Street Station.

It was not very long, days rather than weeks, before another buff envelope arrived at breakfast time. I opened it with some excitement. I was accepted for entry to the Administrative Grade of the Home Civil Service and should report within the next few days to the Establishment Officer of the Department of Health for Scotland, St. Andrew's House, Edinburgh, with a view to starting work as soon as possible. The pleasure and satisfaction at this successful outcome of my series of encounters with the Civil Service Commission was only slightly affected by the awareness that my final Honours examination was due to take place in about six weeks time. A quick letter to the Commission informing them of this and affirming my eagerness to report immediately thereafter would no doubt get everything nicely sorted out.

My quick letter elicited an equally quick but extremely terse reply. If I did not report immediately for work at the Department of Health I would forfeit the appointment. I was astonished that the Civil Service was in such desperate need of my services that it could not wait for six weeks while I rounded off four years of University work by sitting my degree exams. But the tone of the missive did not suggest that the writer was likely to be receptive to further argument. A friend in St. Andrew's House suggested that an approach to the Establishment Officer might be more helpful than further argument with the Commission. So it was. When I saw the Establishment Officer, I was prepared to start work immediately on the basis that I might have time off to do my exams — even though this would mean that the next few weeks, coping with a new job and revising four years of academic work, would be hectic. But I had a receptive and sympathetic audience. That would not be necessary. I should come to the office prepared to start work on the first Monday after the end of my exams; and I should leave the Civil Service Commission to him.

My first discussion in St. Andrew's House could not have had a more successful outcome. For the next few weeks the question of my serving the state in post-war Britain took second place to understanding and appraising events and people in Ancient Greece, in medieval England and in nineteenth century Germany. I heard no more from the Civil Service Commission.

Much later I asked my Establishment colleague how he had managed to silence the Commission. What compelling argument had he deployed? He had in fact done nothing; and, lo, everything had sorted itself out.

Chapter 2

Apprentice in Housing

One Monday morning in June 1947, I reported for duty at the Department of Health for Scotland in St. Andrew's House, Edinburgh. My final honours examination had ended only five days before (and, as I later learned, had produced the hoped-for first). I was told I was to join one of the housing divisions of the Department; but on that day the people concerned were involved in a series of meetings and would be unable to receive me properly. It had been arranged that I would spend the day in the Department's Registry; I would see how incoming correspondence was dealt with and would learn something of the general filing system.

I spent a far from exhilarating day under the care of an elderly clerk, distinguished more for his knowledge of departmental lore than for his professional motivation. In the course of our exploration of the filing system, he told me that the Civil Service was not what it had been before the war. Then the office had closed at 4.00 p.m. As some Registry staff had come in half an hour earlier than the normal starting time to have the mail opened and sent to Divisions, they had left a corresponding half hour earlier in the afternoon. You could be on the tee at 4 o'clock! But it was not like that now. We sat it out until closing time at 5.30.

Next morning I was introduced to the head of the branch in which I was to work, and to the junior staff, all two of them. A desk, vacated by another assistant principal who had moved elsewhere, already awaited me, and some files sat expectantly upon it. The head of branch, James Hogarth, was a principal in his early thirties; he had started as an assistant principal in the spacious pre-war days, spent some years in uniform and returned to the rigours of the post-war Civil Service. He described what was done in the branch and how it fitted in to the general housing responsibilities of the Department. He also gave me some literature and referred to some files which I should read as background. In a day or two he would give me some jobs which I would do under his guidance. I returned to my desk and set to work as an official of the Secretary of State for Scotland.

The Secretary of State was a member of the Cabinet, responsible, along with his junior ministers, for a number of government functions in Scotland — housing, health, education, police, agriculture and others — for each of which a separate minister was responsible in England and Wales. The 'Scottish Office' of which he was in charge consisted in fact of four separate government departments of which the Department of Health for Scotland was one. At the head of each department was a senior civil servant called 'the Secretary' who was responsible to the Secretary of State, usually through the junior minister concerned, for all the Department's work. In order to help the Secretary of State to co-ordinate the activities of these separate departments and to advise him on Scottish matters generally, there was a yet more senior civil servant known as the Permanent Under Secretary of State for Scotland. (This is still in essentials the basic pattern of the Scottish Office today, except that there are now six separate departments. This reflects the extension of the Secretary of State's responsibilities as functions have been transferred from Whitehall departments, and also the formation of one department in the Scottish Office known as Central Services to provide certain common services for the other five.)

At this point it might be helpful to those unfamiliar with the names of the grades at the senior levels in the Civil Service — and there is no reason why 99% of the population should be knowledgeable in such arcane matters — if I set out some basic information. It is no easier to avoid reference to grades in a tale about the Civil Service than it is to avoid reference to captains and majors in an account of life in the army. I have already referred to a 'principal' and to a 'Secretary'. Familiarity with the ordinary meaning of words in the English language is no help to understanding that the former is a good deal junior to the latter; nor does it make it self-evident that the 'Administrative' grades are more senior than the 'Executive' grades. I shall try to keep it simple.

In the early post-war years, as in the pre-war years, most civil servants employed in what in everyday language would be called administrative or clerical work were grouped into three Classes — Administrative, Executive and Clerical. (A few departments, such as the Inland Revenue for example, had their own grading structures; but let us not be involved in these complications.)

Recruits to the service entered one or other of these Classes in the most junior grade. Examinations for entry demanded different levels of educational achievement. The Administrative Class was recruited from the universities; entrants to the Executive Class would normally have had a full secondary education; Clerical entrants need not have spent so long in secondary school. Most of those in the Administrative Class were employed at the headquarters of government departments. It was their job to assist ministers in the formulation of policy and so to run the government machine that ministers' policies were carried out. Members of the Executive Class were generally concerned with the day-to-day implementation of government policy in particular fields, for example at local offices handling applications for some form of financial support. The Clerical Class did ordinary clerical and typing work. Not everyone in the headquarters office of a government department was, of course, in the Administrative Class. Clerical work had to be done there as everywhere else; and members of the Executive Class were often employed in support of those in the Administrative Class. (In industry those at the top levels of an organisation are known as 'executives'. Not so in the Civil Service.)

There were several grades in each Class. The upper grades in the Executive and Clerical Classes were senior to, and much more highly paid than, the lower grades in the Class above (so that, for example, many members of the Executive grades were senior to and much better paid than the lowly recruits to the Administrative Class). The class structure was far from rigid. People could move into a higher Class either by ordinary promotion or as a result of internal examination. Many members of the Administrative Class, for example, had started in the Executive or Clerical Class and worked their way up.

The Administrative class hierarchy of which I was now a very junior member consisted of the following grades in descending order of seniority:

> permanent secretary (in Departments where the Minister was a 'Secretary of State' the permanent secretary was known as 'Permanent Under Secretary of State)
> deputy secretary
> under secretary
> assistant secretary
> principal
> assistant principal

In a typical department there was, and is, one permanent secretary and perhaps two or more deputy secretaries. Each of the latter might be responsible for,

11

according to the nature of the work, three or four under secretaries; and similarly under secretaries and assistant secretaries would have three or four members of the next lower grade 'reporting', as the jargon had it, to them. A principal would not have more than one assistant principal; but since the assistant principal grade was a training grade and the numbers were small — much smaller than the total number of principals — most principals were assisted by a higher executive officer and junior staff.

The Scottish Office as a whole with its Permanent Under Secretary of State was analogous to a major Whitehall department — except that, as I have indicated, the Secretaries of individual departments reported direct to the Secretary of State. These 'Secretaries' in fact ranked as deputy secretaries in the general Civil Service hierarchy.

It will be noted how often the word 'secretary' appears in the hierarchy. This can sometimes lead to confusion on the part of those not used to Civil Service practice. An assistant secretary, far from being a performer of lowly, clerk-like functions, is a man, or woman, of some seniority. (We lack in the English language a personal pronoun singular which applies to both sexes; and therefore on the basis of the old gag that 'man' embraces 'woman', and for more practical reasons of simplicity, I shall refer from now on to civil servants as 'he' when the singular is indicated.) He corresponds to a senior manager in industry. If a junior minister is meeting a deputation, it is as likely as not an assistant secretary who sits at his right hand and who has been responsible for briefing him. The word 'secretary' has been used for centuries to refer to a person with responsibility for some aspect of government. Pepys was Secretary of the Navy in the seventeenth century. There were two Secretaries of State in the eighteenth century. Down the years, as government business expanded, secretaries acquired deputies and assistants; and so the present senior hierarchy of the Civil Service evolved with the word 'secretary' being used along with adjectives such as 'permanent' or 'assistant' to describe a grade rather than a function.

But 'secretary' is also used in the Civil Service as elsewhere to describe a function. A secretary, or a personal secretary, is someone, usually female, who acts as the right hand of a more senior person, keeping his papers, arranging his diary and doing his typing. Ministers as heads of departments have more elaborate arrangements for ordering their activities and the flow of paper. They usually have a 'private office' which consists of a 'private secretary', normally a member of one of the administrative grades, and supporting secretarial and clerical staff. Senior ministers even run to 'principal private secretaries', one private secretary of the administrative variety not being enough. The principal private secretary to the Prime Minister is a very senior administrative civil servant; the private secretary to a junior minister is a very lowly one.

A principal sounds as if he is much grander than any of these. But, as is seen from the table above, a principal is junior to an assistant secretary. This came about as, many years ago, he who is now a principal was called 'principal clerk'. The dropping of the noun was reasonable enough. The principal is not a clerk; he is probably equivalent to a middle grade manager. If an assistant secretary sits at the minister's right hand when receiving a deputation, a principal may well sit at his left hand; and he has almost certainly prepared the draft of the brief which lies on the table in front of each of them.

This brings us to the assistant principal, the lowliest form of life in the Administrative Class when I joined the Civil Service and for many years thereafter. Although it was a training grade, there was no formal arrangement for training. The principal was responsible for giving the AP, as he was known, jobs which would develop basic skills such as summarising complex sets of papers and drafting letters and minutes, and which would extend his understanding of the problems with which the department had to deal. Nowadays, the system is different, and there are much more elaborate arrangements for training. The name 'assistant principal' has disappeared and new entrants are now called 'administration trainees'. (What's in a name? Quite a lot, in the sense that there are the implications for today's entrants which are no part of my tale.)

Alongside the administrative hierarchy in most departments there were, and are, other hierarchies for specialists of various kinds — architects, doctors, lawyers or other professionally or scientifically qualified people, depending on the department's field of activity. There are various grades in these hierarchies usually corresponding to a grade in the administrative hierarchy. But more of this important question of the professional and the administrator later.

Where, or who, it may be asked, are the mandarins of which one hears from time to time in the press? No one is likely to be so innocent as to suppose that there are grades or individuals so described. But to whom are the journalists referring when they speak of the mandarins of the Civil Service? I cannot, of course, answer that question with any assurance, and it is unlikely that those who use the term would be able to offer any precise definition. The term 'mandarin' is a common alternative to 'top civil servant', another ambiguous term occasionally tossed about. Who are these 'top civil servants'? Not only, I think, the permanent secretaries; nor, on the other hand, are they all those

13

including principals and assistant principals in what was once the Administrative Class. There is now a 'Top Salaries Review Committee' which makes recommendations about the salaries of civil servants in the grades of under secretary and above, including professional equivalents. It may be reasonable to think of the members of this top group as the mandarins. One thing is certain: no definition will be found in any official publication.

If you are still with me after that description of grades and hierarchies, you may be glad to return to the Department of Health for Scotland, although DHS, as it was known, was not one of the better known parts of the great British bureaucracy. At some stage in the entry competition, candidates had been asked to indicate in order of preference the departments in which they would like to serve. I had at that time no strong likes or dislikes on that subject (though I acquired a few in the course of my career) but I thought that I ought for a time at least to take the road south. For a historian interested in government there was a certain glamour about Whitehall and Westminster, at least as seen from a distance by reading books and newspapers. I had put down the Treasury, the Ministry of Health and the Scottish Office, in that order. The Treasury was the hub of Government, involved in the activities of all departments; the Ministry of Health covered a wide variety of functions of obvious value to the citizen — housing, health, water and sewage and town and country planning. And the Scottish Office? If I were not wanted for either of the first two there were attractions in joining an organisation responsible for many government activities on my home territory. In the event, it was presumably a clerk in the Civil Service Commission who when faced with two papers — a list of successful applicants and a list of departments to which they were to be sent — decided to combine my second and third choice.

Like the Ministry of Health, the DHS dealt not only with questions of public health, which in 1947 included planning for a new National Health Service, but with two other subjects with which earlier governments had had to concern themselves because of their health implications — housing, and water and sewerage. It also dealt with another closely-related subject: town and country planning. By 1947, the government's interest in housing had moved far beyond its health implications. Hardly any houses had been built during the war, and many new houses were needed urgently simply for people to live in. The general policy branch of the housing side of the Department dealt with general policy across the board — the arrangements for the construction of new houses by local authorities, the various forms of financial support, modernisation and improvement of houses, control of private building. Between the wars about three quarters of new houses in Scotland had been built by local authorities. In the immediate post-war period this proportion was greatly increased as the government concentrated on the building of houses to let, and private building was restricted. When it became apparent late in 1947 that the number of houses being started was out-running the available supplies of labour and materials, it was the general policy branch which had to consider how to put on the brakes.

Other housing branches considered, along with the architects and surveyors, the detailed proposals for plans of local authorities, and approved, rejected or amended them. The need for departmental scrutiny was taken for granted in those days as it was assumed the government ought to see and approve exactly what was being provided with the help of Exchequer Funds. (The sceptic might wonder when looking at some of the dreary housing schemes built at that time whether they could have been any worse if local authorities, who after all provided some of the funds and employed architects as well qualified as those in government departments, had been allowed to build without supervision.) Another branch dealt with the various forms of non-traditional building being developed at that time. If satisfied that new methods would speed the provision of acceptable new houses, they commended them to local authorities. When I saw unfamiliar sharp-suited gentlemen walking along the corridor, it was a fair chance that they were promoters and developers of non-traditional houses.

What did all this involve for a new boy like me? Recent papers on some problem had to be summarised for my principal. A letter from a local authority raising a general point might be discussed with him, and then I would tentatively draft a reply for him to send. Policy issues of importance involved the assistant secretary and the under secretary. There would be office meetings and I would draft a minute of the discussion. (I soon learned that in the Civil Service the most junior person at a meeting drafts the minutes — though higher authority may want to see and perhaps amend them before the final version is circulated.) When building costs rose alarmingly, the Secretary of State appointed an independent committee on Scottish Building Costs. James Hogarth was appointed secretary and I became *de facto* assistant secretary, arranging places to meet, circulating papers and, of course, drafting the minutes.

I was introduced to two types of official business which can land on administrators' desks until the day they retire — ministerial correspondence and Parliamentary Questions. (For some reason the latter and their Answers are always dignified by capital letters.)

Ministers receive correspondence from many quarters. Letters from unknown individuals are usually passed to the department to send a reply on behalf of the minister. It would be a very unusual minister who did not want to reply himself to letters from constituents, from important organisations and individuals with whom he is in personal contact, and from Members of Parliament. Letters from the latter arrive in large numbers, for MPs are eager to pass on to ministers for comment or help letters they receive from their constituents. If the constituent is criticising government policy, the MP expects a ministerial explanation; if the constituent says that he is being oppressed or denied his rights, the MP expects the minister to do something about it. In any event, he wants a reply which he can send to his constituent with such comments of his own — tart, grateful, deferential or derisive — as he thinks appropriate. Ministers understandably look to the department for helpful draft replies to all their letters.

Generally the minister's private office puts each one in a special folder, immediately recognisable as containing ministerial correspondence. This is sent to the department for a draft reply to be available by a specified date. The level in the departmental hierarchy at which the final draft, which might be the first draft unchanged, the first draft amended, or some new version altogether, is cleared for submission to the minister may vary according to departmental practice and the importance of the issue.

In the Scottish Office folders containing ministerial correspondence were an eye-catching shade of green; and even in my early days these green folders came regularly on to my desk for a first shot at a reply. If the letter raised a general point on which the government's line was clear, it was not difficult to decide on the content. If, occasionally, a new point was raised, the draft could suggest the answer. If this was acceptable to higher authority and to the minister a tiny area of government policy would have been defined. The style and tone of these replies might depend to some extent on whether the letter came from a political supporter or opponent. Generally, unless the minister was a very abrasive type or for some reason a very robust reply seemed called for, departmental drafts addressed themselves in as helpful a way as possible to the issues raised, avoiding any temptation to make debating points. The aim was to reveal the sender, the minister, as understanding, reasonable and sympathetic and, if unable to accede to a request, eager to explain why. If not all ministers personally were understanding, reasonable and sympathetic, the unspoken assumption was that officially, as ministers, they ought to be.

Much ministerial correspondence deals with particular cases. In the general policy branch the only kind of individual cases which came my way were those concerned with the issue or non-issue of licences to build private houses. The issue of these licences was the responsibility of local authorities; but from early 1948 as part of the restrictions on new building work, they could be issued only with the agreement of the Secretary of State, which in practice meant the Department. Each proposal was solemnly considered by a small group of which I was the secretary. Very often rejection of an application led to a letter from an MP to the minister. In the draft replies which I put forward there had to be an explanation of the reasons why new building work was being restricted and the priorities against which ministers had decided applications should be considered. The recipients, I thought, were unlikely to be convinced that the construction or improvement of their particular houses would endanger the success of the post-war housing effort; and I tried to temper my recital of government policy with as much sympathy and understanding as I could muster.

It was always interesting to get back the folders of ministerial correspondence after the minister had written, and a copy of his letter had been placed on top of the file. From the papers below I would see whether my draft had been altered higher in the Department before it had reached him and whether he had accepted the final departmental draft. As the weeks went by what I came to regard as my success rate improved, and my drafts would survive with only slight alteration. Conversation with other APs showed that as much would depend on the habits and attitudes of one's principal — did he, for example, tinker with drafts in order to make 'improvements' which were apparent to him but to no one else? — as on the skill of the trainee. Ministers were not much interested in the niceties of drafting; if the suggested reply conveyed the message they wanted to convey — and it usually did, for their views and policies were well understood — they left well alone.

Ministerial correspondence, however important, is just a particular kind of ordinary correspondence. Parliamentary Questions, the other special type of business to which I was soon introduced, have no analogues outside government departments. In some of the older text books about the government of Britain, the Parliamentary Question is almost venerated as one of the pillars of our liberties, and even in these more cynical days, newspaper readers are expected to be suitably impressed when it is reported that an MP full of concern about this or that is going to put down a Question in Parliament. The less

17

sophisticated may well suppose that if knees were not actually knocking, hearts are beating faster in the corridors of power.

In fact, as I soon learned, Parliamentary Questions, or PQs as they are known, far from being awesome and infrequent, are an ordinary routine part of departmental business during the Parliamentary session. There are, however, two reasons why they have to be handled with special care and attention. First, they are put down to be answered on a particular day, either orally or in written form, and this means that whatever other business may have to be put aside, a draft reply and supporting material has to be in the minister's hands a day or so before. Second, even if the Questions themselves are not particularly difficult, the circumstances in which oral Answers are given, especially to members of the Opposition, can sometimes produce high drama — or low farce. The minister stands up in the House before what is at best a group of people eager to catch him out, and at worst a hostile mob. He has to give a reply to the original Question — which does not tax him as he merely reads a prepared reply — but then he has to reply to supplementary questions thrown at him without notice. This can sometimes be very testing indeed. He has to give answers on the spot in such a way that if possible his reputation will be enhanced or at least that he will not be torn to shreds. The notes before him which he has studied carefully beforehand can be crucially important even for the most nimble and sure-footed of ministers. Against this background, these notes have be be prepared in the department with both care and imagination, and usually the Secretary himself will want to be satisfied that they are as good as they can be.

When the text of a PQ was received in DHS, it was typed and filed in a special folder, even more eye-catching than the type of folder used for ministerial correspondence. It was then passed down by hand from the Secretary's Private Office to the level in the division concerned at which someone would decide, or be told, that he had to make a start on it. This could be a fairly junior level; and it was not long after my arrival that my principal came in bearing one of these folders and indicating the lines on which I should have a go.

As part of my indoctrination in my first few days I had studied one or two folders of past Questions and seen the form in which material was prepared for the minister. For Questions to which the MP wanted an oral Answer, the material had to be put forward in three parts. First, a suggested reply for the minister to read out. This was usually quite short, if possible one or two sentences, no more. Second, there were what were called 'Notes for Supplementaries'. Here, departmental officials knowing the strengths and weaknesses of the policy, having found out whether there were any particular problems in the MP's constituency, and thinking how they themselves might most effectively get under the minister's guard if they were sitting on the other side of the House, had set out possible supplementary questions and possible Answers. Finally, there were 'background notes'. These described the general background from which the Question arose — the general policy, and any relevant legislation or departmental circulars, the history of the case (if the Question concerned a particular case). Sometimes there was some overlapping between notes for supplementaries and background notes, but there was no harm in that. If an oral reply was not wanted, the notes for supplementaries were omitted. Quite often, Question Time in the House was not long enough for all oral Questions to be answered. If time was up before an oral Answer could be given, the written text of the Answer was given to the Member.

Working on this pattern I made my first attempt. It was not highly thought of by my principal and he recast most of it — suggested reply and all the rest. As further Questions flowed in, my performance improved; but my success rate, at least as far as the suggested Answer was concerned, was never as high as it was with ministerial correspondence. I found the APs in other parts of the office had a similar experience; and as I saw more and more of these folders, those belonging to other branches as well as my own, I realised that the principal's score was not particularly high either. Nor was the assistant secretary's. It dawned on me that nearly everyone at all stages in the hierarchy in all parts of the office fancied himself as a drafter of neat Answers. It was regarded as a minor art form, the supreme test of a civil servant's drafting skill. While senior officials were often content to let other kinds of drafts go by if the right thing was said, albeit in language less effective or elegant than they themselves might have used, suggested replies to PQs were different. The words of these replies would go from the minister's very lips into the ears of ill-disposed persons eager to twist them to their own advantage. They had to be the best possible form of words, the words the senior officer himself would use. And so thought *his* senior in turn, when the folder landed on his desk. So the draft reply might be changed again, though notes for supplementaries and background notes often survived unscathed. Ministers accepted most draft replies; they were less interested in the linguistic arts than their officials.

There was seldom much doubt about the message which an Answer should convey. Sometimes the questioner would ask whether the minister would do something which he knew the minister was most unlikely to do — because it was contrary to current policy or because more finance would be required.

Sometimes the minister would be asked to reverse a decision recently taken. But no minister was likely to do that just because he was being pressed by his opponents; he had expected that reaction when he made his decision. There is a kind of ritual dance about much Parliamentary activity. MPs know the kind of reply they will get to most Questions, but their 'pressure on the minister' looks good when reported in the local newspaper.

In preparing material for Questions, officials' doubts are more likely to relate to the tone and emphasis of draft replies. How exactly should what is undoubtedly a brush-off be phrased? Politely or curtly? If the reply has to undertake to consider representations being made, how forthcoming should it be?

In 1947–48 when there was general concern about getting the maximum number of houses built as soon as possible, the Questions kept flowing in. Towards the end of one week when, most unusually, both my principal and the assistant secretary were away, no fewer than eleven Questions landed on my desk. They all had to be fully cleared in the Department that week in preparation for Scottish Questions on the following Tuesday. After a good deal of effort, I sent eleven folders complete with suggested replies and supporting material to the under secretary, Craig Mitchell, a genial fatherly figure who had started his career as a boy clerk. His geniality did not extend to admiration of other people's prose, and he was well known for his automatic reaching for his pen whenever a draft floated under his eyes. I was asked to go and see him. He said in a kindly way that I had done quite a good job, but I seemed to be rather intolerant of some of the Questions. He acknowledged that some of them were indeed pretty stupid, but I must not let this reaction show in my draft answers. He showed me how he had changed and elaborated some of the answers to be less terse and more apparently forthcoming without actually saying anything more than I had. When in reply to one Question asking whether the minister would do something which was clearly a non-starter, I had suggested the reply, 'No, sir', he had substituted a rather flowery sentence on the lines of 'Bearing in mind . . . it would not be appropriate at present to . . .' I said 'No, sir' was by no means an uncommon reply. He agreed, but it all depended on the circumstances, and he thought it too abrupt in answer to that particular MP. He was quite right. I undertook to take his words to heart; and I did — with only a few silent reservations.

The nearest thing to centrally organised training for APs in these days was a two week course at the Treasury. About a year after my arrival in DHS I joined about twenty other APs from other departments in a back room in the rabbit warren which was the old Treasury Building in Whitehall. There were talks about Parliamentary procedure as it affected us, the Cabinet Office and various aspects of government organisation; we had exercises in drafting — particularly Answers to Parliamentary Questions. It was helpful, informative, urbane and undemanding.

Apart from that I was given opportunities now and again to leave my desk and see the Department and its work from a different angle. I spent a day sitting in the visitors' gallery at the annual conference of the Scottish Trades Union Conference listening to a flow of rhetoric and prejudice — educative, I suppose, in a way. A week on the road in the Highlands with one of the Department's housing inspectors was educative in another way. We tramped over muddy housing sites and met local authority officials and contractors. We visited one large mansion and one or two cottages where the owners were seeking licences for work to repair years of neglect.

But most of the time I was in the office. If in my gloomier moments I found the constraints of working at a lowly level in an organisation rather dispiriting, especially after the freedom and wider intellectual horizons of the University, I accepted this as part of the reality of earning a living. On the whole I enjoyed the work and found it interesting. And I found it interesting, too, to contemplate the physical and social environment in which I found myself.

St. Andrew's House, set on the south side of the Calton Hill a couple of hundred yards from the east end of Princes Street, was a splendid 1930s building completed just before the war. While occasional trams clattered along Regent Road on the north side between the front of the building and the steep slope of the hill, nothing disturbed the peace of the rooms at the back except the occasional toots and hisses of the trains entering or leaving the Waverley Station far below. These were the most desirable rooms with a magnificent view over the Old Town of Edinburgh and the Castle and the Pentland Hills beyond. Years later, connoisseurs of Art Deco would delight in many of the building's internal mouldings and fittings — and more worldly characters would find themselves plagued by draughts as the metal-framed windows began to buckle and let in the cold winds from the North Sea. Meanwhile it was a pleasant place to work — bright, airy and spacious.

Most senior staff sat in rooms on the south side, assistant secretaries and above having rooms to themselves, and principals sharing. After I had spent a while on the north side, those responsible for matching bodies to accommodation decided that I should move. A room on the south side had been vacant for some time because of the illness of its normal occupant, an assistant secretary. Pressure on accommodation was increasing and I would sit in this assistant secretary's room at his desk until his return. For some weeks I enjoyed a standard of accommodation and furniture to which I was unaccustomed and which I would not again savour for many years. When the assistant secretary made a tentative return to the office for a couple of hours each morning he said there was no question of my moving out. Another desk was brought in and for some weeks my mornings were enlivened by anecdotes and reminiscences.

Alec Riddet was a friendly couthy Scot from Glasgow. He had been Depute Town Clerk of that city before the war, and during the war had been Food Officer for the area. Then he had been invited to join DHS to help liaison with local authorities in the post-war housing drive. A severe heart-attack had struck him down and he had been laid aside for many months. Still frail and far from fit, his return to the office was clearly intended more as a boost to his morale than a serious resumption of responsibility. But his brain was sharp, his memory clear and he enjoyed talking to a young man about some of the more colourful aspects of local government administration. Fascinated by his tales about councillors, contractors and the Glasgow citizenry, I did nothing to discourage him. He came in one morning saying, 'It's a great thing, James, to be able to get up in the morning and go to your work.' A few days later he did not appear; he had had another heart attack. Soon we learned that he had died. The room seemed very empty without him.

The accommodation men were not long in making new arrangements. I was moved on to share a room with an elderly principal. When my room-mate came in on the first morning, he whipped off his black Homburg hat and dark overcoat; off came the jacket of his smart grey suit and he donned a shiny crumpled jacket which had been hanging overnight on a peg. He was now ready for action. Most of his generation in the middle and lower grades had these 'office jackets' which were worn at the desk to save wear and tear on their everyday suits. Nothing much could be done about trousers except that shine on the seat could be avoided by putting cushions on leather chairs. For meetings with visitors and very senior officers, office jackets were returned to the peg and the trim smartness of the suit was restored. Office jackets varied in colour, material and degree of deterioration. One eccentric character sported a jacket which was in the final stages of disintegration. Leather patches which had been sewn on the elbows now threatened to fly off when he moved; and leather bindings round the cuffs had almost parted company with the sleeves so that he seemed to have two bangles bouncing on his wrists.

While the majority of the staff, male and female, wore hats, no one seemed concerned that some young males, including myself, arrived and departed hatless. There were no rules about dress in the office, but the conventions were strong. Men, however junior, arrived in suits and except in the hottest days of summer none was seen without a jacket, however battered. The prospect of any women wearing trousers was far from anyone's imagining. On Saturday mornings — the five-day week was yet to come — convention allowed that especially in summer men could wear sports jackets and flannels so as to make a quick escape to the golf course, the hills or the seaside.

The office canteen on the top floor was well patronised. In these days of food rationing menus were rich in rissoles, 'Cambridge steaks' (and other fancy descriptions for amalgams of the left-overs of yesterday and the day before), sausages and fish pies. But it was all quite acceptable, granted the standards to which everyone was accustomed, and lunch was an occasion to meet colleagues and extend one's acquaintance in other departments. I even began to recognise the awesome personages who were the heads of the departments. The sense of hierarchy which dominated our official relationships did not determine all arrangements in St. Andrew's House; and there was only one canteen shared by all. Democracy ruled, too, in the lavatories, where the only distinction was between 'men' and 'women', not, be it noted, 'ladies' and 'gentlemen'.

The weeks and months went steadily by. I knew that sooner rather than later I would be transferred to some other field of work since APs were moved from time to time to gain experience. One day in the spring of 1949 I was told I was to be appointed private secretary to the Parliamentary Under Secretary of State.

Chapter 3

Minister's Private Secretary

I had spent almost two years in the Department, and the shadows of ministers had never been far away. I had prepared drafts, albeit oft-rejected first drafts, of their Answers to Parliamentary Questions; I had put forward suggested replies to their incoming letters; I had contributed to the briefing material for their meetings; I had seen copies of their signatures on letters; I had even caught sight of them emerging from their cars at the front door. But I had never actually met a real live minister and seen the whites of his eyes.

Now I had been nominated by the Department for appointment as private secretary to one of the figures casting these omnipresent shadows. One day in the late spring of 1949 I was escorted by Craig Mitchell to the office of Mr J. J. Robertson, MP, Parliamentary Under Secretary of State for Scotland. On the way I was told that ministers normally accepted whoever the Department suggested for appointment as private secretaries; but it was only reasonable that they should have the chance to cast their eyes over the nominee and talk to him before the decision was finally made. Now Mr Robertson was going to have a look at me and presumably consider whether he could bear the prospect of having me at his elbow every day.

In the minister's room we had a few minutes of pleasant chat very different from the kind of inquisition to which I had been subjected when interviewed at the Civil Service Commission. 'J.J.', as he was known, must have found the sight and sound of me at least tolerable for we went on to settle arrangements for my formal appointment. I then saw my predecessor, destined to return to the Department on promotion, and we arranged to have a few days working together so that I could learn the ropes of the private office — and the likes, dislikes, habits and peculiarities of my new boss.

25

Then, as now, Scottish Office ministers — in those days only the Secretary of State and two Parliamentary Under Secretaries — spent most of the week during the Parliamentary session in London. They were, after all, Members of Parliament and had to be available for ordinary Parliamentary as well as ministerial duties. They left home usually on a Sunday evening and travelled by night sleeper to London, returning overnight on Thursdays. Fridays and Saturday mornings were available for meetings and visits in Scotland and work in St. Andrew's House. Before the war the Scottish Office had had its London headquarters in Dover House, a historic eighteenth century mansion house in Whitehall. They had been ejected during the war; and while there were hopes of a return to the traditional home, they were housed for the present in Fielden House in Great College Street, a quiet backwater only five minutes walk from the House. There was accommodation for the ministers, their private secretaries and supporting London based clerical staff. In that building, too, each department of the Scottish Office had a small liaison staff, of one or two people, whose job it was to keep in touch with the corresponding English Department and represent the Scottish department at London meetings when it was not essential to have the experts from Edinburgh.

I started my new job with enthusiasm tempered by awe. I would now be close to the seat of power; I would see history being made; I would help in a very small way to make some big things happen. Private secretary jobs, according to departmental lore, were for up-and-coming young men; it was a great honour to be selected. What better job could there be for a young civil servant in the early days of his career?

The few days with my predecessor, some in Edinburgh, some in London, were soon over. I was not quite on my own as the private secretaries to all three ministers shared large rooms in Edinburgh and London with their supporting staff. But at first it was frightening as well as exhilarating. When the telephone rang — and it seldom seemed to stop — it was more likely to be the Cabinet office, an MP or the head of a department than, as in my housing days, a colleague from along the corridor. Too often I seemed to fumble and mumble my hesitant replies. The other private secretaries seemed very assured in telling their callers how their ministers would react to this or that. I got lost when trying to find my way through the labyrinth of corridors of the Palace of Westminster to my minister's room. But after a couple of very busy weeks during which it seemed I had not got the minister or myself in trouble, I began to feel if not confident at least a good deal less apprehensive in my dealings with enquirers, high and low, and with the minister himself.

J.J. was by birth a Shetlander. He had served in the Royal Navy and after the war had been a member of Edinburgh Town Council. He did not seem to have any outstanding qualities to mark him out for high office and mention in the history books. For a politician, judging from what I knew of politicians at second-hand, he seemed fairly easy-going, showing no strong personal ambition or desire to change the world. He was not a difficult master, but I soon learned that one of his most urgent priorities was so to arrange his diary and his transport that he could escape from London each Thursday at the earliest possible time. If there was one mystery about him, it was why he had been singled out for office from the considerable number of Scottish Labour MPs in that first post-war Parliament.

The Secretary of State was Arthur Woodburn, an avuncular figure, who was a leading figure in the Labour Party in Scotland. The other Parliamentary Secretary was Tom Fraser who had a charm of manner not always associated with ex-miners from Lanarkshire. While the ministers divided up the responsibilities of the Scottish Office between them — J.J. had the Fisheries responsibilities of the Scottish Home Department as well as all the responsibilities of DHS — the Secretary of State was in overall command, and they acted as a team deputising for one another. So it was too with their private secretaries. We were each primarily responsible to our own minister, but we too often had to cover for each other. Indeed, Tom Fraser's PS and I were officially designated as assistant private secretaries to the Secretary of State.

The job of the PS varies to some extent with the minister — how energetic he is, how much briefing he wants or needs (which may be different), whether he promotes new policies or whether he tends more to react to events. But the basic nature of most of the work does not change. The PS is responsible for the minister's diary — considering requests for him to see deputations, fixing dates for visits to new developments or problem spots in various parts of the country, negotiating with private secretaries in other departments about times for ministerial meetings, arranging times for senior officials to come to brief him — consulting the minister himself when necessary, seeking departmental advice when needed and always bearing in mind inescapable Parliamentary commitments. The PS must ensure that written briefs for meetings are to hand in good time, that answers are obtained to all the minister's questions, that the minister's correspondence is kept flowing evenly, that cars are ordered and appear on time — and that the minister himself appears on time.

With the general run of the minister's ordinary Parliamentary activities — for example, being in the House to vote according to the Whip on matters not connected with the department — the PS is hardly concerned at all, though such commitments do affect freedom of manoeuvre for ministerial business. Nor is he concerned with Party or constituency matters. How far he may hear about or be brought into the minister's personal affairs — his family, his finances, his digestion — depends on the minister, the PS and the relationship which develops between them.

The PS is very much concerned with those Parliamentary activities in which the minister is involved because of his office. Of these, the most onerous and time-consuming is probably the making of new legislation — carrying a Bill through its various stages until it becomes an Act of Parliament. Sometimes a department may have no legislation of any consequence before the House, but when I joined J.J. he was already involved in piloting a Housing (Scotland) Bill through its committee stage. This Bill was principally concerned to authorise the making of grants for the improvement of existing houses, but it also dealt with a number of miscellaneous housing matters.

I was reasonably familiar at second hand with the more important aspects of Parliamentary procedure. I knew that during the debate on the second reading of this Bill on the floor of the House its main principles would have been discussed, and that now at committee stage the Bill would be considered line by line and amendments considered. This examination of Scottish Bills was always considered by the Scottish Grand Committee consisting of all Members of the House of Commons representing Scottish constituencies, with some other Members added so as to reflect the party balance of the whole House. But text-books and official papers, in their austere way, and even newspaper reports, had not prepared me for the general atmosphere and ethos of the Scottish Grand Committee on the first occasion I accompanied J.J. to one of its morning meetings.

At first there were few Members present except for the official spokesmen of Government and Opposition. Gradually as the discussion went on, Members drifted in, greeting their colleagues and apparently paying no attention to whoever was speaking. They would sit down at one of the long tables, open up their brief-cases and empty out an assemblage of papers and envelopes. Then out would come some instrument to open the envelopes, and soon the Member was ready to look through his morning mail. He would occasionally stop his perusal or his writing to listen when some vibrations told him that an important, controversial or amusing point was being made; but then he would return to the real work of the morning. Only a minority of those present followed the debate closely or took part; for the majority, without a desk or a room of their own in

28

the vast Palace of Westminster, this committee room was as much an office as a debating chamber. When a vote was called, it was not difficult to follow the front bench spokesman.

The Committee met on two mornings each week from 10.30 until 1 o'clock. There was a small team of officials from Edinburgh sitting not in an 'official box' as in the House itself but at the chairman's right hand at the top table, within an arm's length of the minister's seat at the end of one of the long tables set at right angles. There had been briefing sessions on the day before at which minister and officials had gone over the amendments proposed by Members, and sometimes by the Government itself, and had agreed the line to be followed and the points to be made. For each clause and each amendment the minister had before him various notes from which he would speak. But as Members spoke, additional notes would sometimes be handed to him, and he would often move across and have a tête-à-tête with one of the officials.

With a seat behind the departmental team I, like many of the MPs, could get on with some paper work. Sometimes, however, when one of the acknowledged characters was on his feet, it was worth listening. Walter Elliott, elder statesman, former Secretary of State, was a debater of long experience, who, if sometimes a little verbose, could with skill and good humour destroy his opponents' arguments. Sir Will Y. Darling, former Lord Provost of Edinburgh, resplendent in frock coat and striped trousers (with top hat parked not far away), if not a serious debater usually provided some amusement. One clause of the Bill proposed to remove the existing restriction by which local authorities provided housing 'for the working class'; henceforth they would be able to provide housing for anyone. How clever of the government, he thought. To hide the fact that they had failed to provide housing for the working class, they had decided to abolish the working class! The debate on that Bill ground on. Each morning, the earnest, the lightweight, the knowledgeable and the ignorant had their say; and precisely at 1 o'clock the chairman closed that day's session.

There were other Parliamentary duties for the minister. Scottish Questions had to be answered (in those days) on Tuesdays; and from time to time there were debates on one of the subjects for which J.J. was responsible. What the precise occasions were I have long since forgotten. No doubt he replied to Opposition motions that Regulations made by the Secretary of State be withdrawn; and there were debates, I am sure, on general government policy on health or housing, involving English as well as Scottish ministers. To all such occasions the PS had to make his modest contribution — requesting briefs in advance from the department, trying sometimes, when these were received, to persuade a reluctant minister of the strength of the departmental line — or agreeing with him that it needed to be elaborated, reinforced or altered; conveying this to a sometimes sceptical department; arranging briefing sessions at which officials would appear; and keeping contact with private secretaries in English departments so that the minister knew what his opposite numbers in these departments were going to say or do. When the appointed hour for the debate arrived I would go with the officials into the official box and hope for the best.

Propriety and good sense called for a sober demeanour in the box even when we knew Hon. Members were talking rubbish. Restrained amusement at jokes or jibes from the Government side might be acceptable; but it was not prudent to join in when hearty laughter erupted on Opposition benches. Sometimes there would be very useful speeches garnished with wisdom and good sense. But there could be periods of boredom or exasperation. I remember one sorely-tried official bent forward as in prayer with his head between his hands, saying fervently, 'Oh, God; oh, God.' Debates could go on for hours with only a few members dotted about on mainly empty benches. There could be awkward moments. There was never any danger that the minister would lose the vote — the Whips would see to that — but there was always the possibility that he might make some unguarded remark which later would lead to trouble; or some knowledgeable Member would refer to important facts of which the minister was unaware, facts which the Department should have given him in advance. And so there was always a certain relief when the debate closed and we could troop out of the box without having to prepare ourselves for an awkward post-mortem.

After a debate it was common practice for Members or private secretaries on behalf of ministers to go upstairs to the *Hansard* office and check the text of their speeches as recorded by the shorthand writers. There was no question of changing what had been said or deleting something the Member or the minister wished he had not said. But sometimes a place-name in a remote part of Ross and Cromarty had to be spelt out to a completely baffled member of the *Hansard* staff, or some lapse into broad Scots made intelligible. And occasionally, very occasionally, shorthand writers could get it wrong. This would require some delicate diplomacy for *Hansard* staff were very skilled professionals not easily convinced that what they had recorded had not been said.

During my first few weeks I enjoyed the job and the glamour of Westminster. It was exhilarating to rise from my desk in Fielden House, walk for a few minutes on a fine early summer day to the Palace of Westminster and go in by St. Stephen's entrance. In these innocent days no security men barred the way. In I strode (or anyone else for that matter), past a policeman posted apparently to act as guide as much as guard, on with a leftward look into the vastness of Westminster Hall, past the queues of visitors waiting to get into the gallery, and then into the central lobby. Here there was always a great to-ing and fro-ing of MPs, ministers, Parliamentary staff and visitors — some of the latter merely tourists, others earnestly bearing representations, others again anxious for help and some no doubt hoping for a profitable deal. I would make my way through the throng, recognising some famous faces as I headed for the Chamber or the minister's room. If I was challenged by one of the policemen dotted about in the labyrinth of that vast building I would say I was private secretary to Mr J. J. Robertson. He accepted this; he asked for no written confirmation and, apart from a brief-case full of official papers, I had none.

One policeman got to know me very soon, the 'Policeman behind the Chair'. He was always posted just outside the Chamber itself at the entrance which was literally behind the Speaker's Chair. It was not because of any distinctive qualities of mine that he recognised me; he knew everyone who had reason to be in that part of the building — Members, ministers' private secretaries and Parliamentary staff. While the Whips of the two sides normally agreed on the timing of the day's business, the Policeman behind the Chair knew from Members passing in and out of the Chamber whether that time-table was being observed, and if not, why not. Officials and ministerial private secretaries sitting in Whitehall offices, with their ministers incommunicado in the Chamber, could find out what was happening and when the business might require their presence only by ringing the ever obliging Policeman behind the Chair.

By the time the long hot days of July were upon us, the glamour of the job was beginning to fade. More than that, I began to feel slightly dispirited. The job itself was not particularly demanding or stimulating — not so demanding or stimulating as it might have been with an up-and-coming minister. I was, I thought in my gloomier moments, little more than a message boy, albeit a high grade message boy conveying important messages. And these gloomier moments became more frequent as the sticky, humid weather of central London made me long for some fresh Edinburgh air. The private office had to be manned on Saturday mornings even although all the ministers were in

Scotland, and I and my colleague, who was PS to Tom Fraser, had to take turns of spending week-ends in London. This meant we were in London for ten days out of fourteen. Many people might have found such a fate more than welcome, but I found metropolitan life had fewer attractions than I had expected.

To some extent, this disenchantment was my own fault. I had not made any effort to find digs, a flat or some convenient London base. During the war, in order to provide overnight accommodation for officials from Edinburgh when hotel accommodation was short, beds had been set up in all the rooms in Fielden House where space permitted. Only ministers' rooms were excepted — though the Secretary of State's spacious office became from about 9.00 p.m. a Common Room where tea, biscuits and camaraderie were available. These convenient arrangements still lingered on, and many officials from Edinburgh availed themselves of them. It was all too easy for me, without friends or relatives or accustomed resting-places in London, to do likewise. But it was ill-advised. Dossing down over-night on one of these austere metal-framed beds and clearing away all one's things in the morning did not give any sense of belonging or a place one could call one's own. For a night or two now and again it was convenient; for ten nights out of fourteen it was absurd. And so, although it was no part of my intention, I made myself something of a rootless émigré.

Morale revived at the end of July when the beginning of the Parliamentary recess saw ministers setting off on holiday and I was able to take the night train north without thinking I would be back again in a few days. Morale rose even higher when in mid-August I became engaged to be married to a charming young lady in St. Andrew's House. Morale remained high with the prospect later that month of ministerial and private office duties in Scotland of a kind which I had not yet experienced.

It had become traditional in the Scottish Office that during the long summer recess there should be a ministerial tour in some remote part of Scotland using one of the fishery protection vessels. That summer Mr J. J. Robertson was to visit Shetland. Officials from the various departments, those concerned with agriculture and fisheries as well as housing, health and local government, had drawn up a programme and provided the usual volume of briefs for about a week of visits to local authorities, to small communities where developments had been carried out and to other remote places from where for years there had been representations that something had to be done. The oil boom and prosperity had yet to hit the Shetland Isles.

The good ship *Brenda* sailed north from Lerwick past flat windswept islands round to Scalloway on the west of 'Mainland', stopping here and there on the way. From Scalloway we sailed west to the remotest island of the Shetland Group — Foula, a lonely rock in the Atlantic, yet home for a few score hardy souls. We met and talked to some of them, including one cheerful old lady with bright red cheeks burnished by the constant winds. Aboard again, we sailed under the highest cliffs in the British Isles, and watched the sea-birds swooping and planing in the upward currents of air. London was very far away. There were more visits ashore on the southern part of Mainland and adjacent islands. J. J., one or two officials from St. Andrew's House and I would file off the *Brenda*, look at boats, piers and bridges (or places where it was argued piers or bridges ought to be) houses, roads, sheep and cattle. J.J. listened, promised something when he could, explained and sympathised when he could not. All too soon we had rounded Sumburgh Head and were back at Lerwick.

As summer began to give way to autumn, the prospect of heading south loomed up once again. If I had been intending that my bachelor state should be undisturbed, I suppose I would have soldiered on, albeit unenthusiastically. But my fiancée and I hoped to marry fairly soon, and the prospect of my spending ten out of fourteen days in London while she remained in Edinburgh seemed to me no way to start a marriage. I thought I should ask to leave the PS job and return to the Department. She was torn. On the one hand she too was eager that we should start our life together, but she was concerned about the effect of such a decision on my career prospects. In the event, I decided that all things considered the right thing to do was to ask for release; and my career prospects could look after themselves.

J.J. himself was understanding and made no fuss but, as I expected, my request was certainly not welcomed in the Department. There was as much shock and disbelief as disapproval. No PS ever before had asked to return to the Department after only six months. I was doing quite well in the job; why throw away all the opportunities and kudos it offered? My former under-secretary, Craig Mitchell, with whom I had had continued dealings from the private office, spoke to me in a sympathetic way and tried, unsuccessfully, to dissuade me. I was paraded before Sir David Milne, the Permanent Under Secretary of State himself; but by then it was apparent my mind was made up, and he merely expressed surprise and regret. Probably they could have insisted that I continue. But the Department had an obligation to provide for ministers the most suitable private secretaries they could find, and I could now hardly be said to be in that category. There were, after all, other bright, perhaps brighter, young men about. It was agreed that at the beginning of December I should return to the Department.

During the remaining weeks I worked away at Fielden House and Westminster with a lighter heart. Somehow time was found to buy a house in Edinburgh and to make arrangements for a wedding in January. Towards the end of November there was a pleasant ceremony in St. Andrew's House at which J.J. presented to my fiancée and myself, on behalf of those with whom we had worked, a very acceptable wedding present. It was nice to find as she had retired from the Civil Service and I left the private office, even in unusual circumstances, that so many people wished us well.

Chapter 4

Introduction to the National Health Service

In December 1949, once more an ordinary assistant principal shorn of private secretary status and allowance, I joined the part of the Department which was responsible for the administration of the National Health Service.

Legislation to set up the Service had been passed fairly easily in 1946 and 1947 by the large Labour majority in the House of Commons, but there had been major disagreements between the Government and the medical profession about the role, status and remuneration of doctors. At one stage it had seemed doubtful whether the legislation on the statute book would ever be translated into service on the ground. In the event, the majority of doctors were sufficiently persuaded, and on the 'Appointed Day', 5th July 1948, the National Health Service had been brought to birth. It had taken over existing resources of buildings and manpower and, although by the end of 1949 there had been no significant re-planning or development of existing services, the new Service was reasonably well established. It had cost much more in the first year than had been estimated, but the first of the regular crises which were to become an established feature of the British Way of Life — 'Is the NHS about to collapse?' — had been overcome.

I found myself in a branch concerned principally with the pay and conditions of service of hospital medical staff. Among our other responsibilities were the ambulance service and travelling expenses for patients. The principal in charge of the branch was very different in background and administrative style from my first principal in my housing days. While James Hogarth had been a standard entrant to the Administrative Class after university, my new boss had joined the Civil Service during the war after having worked as an accountant abroad. I had in my housing job been accustomed to brief business-like exchanges which seldom strayed from the point at issue. Now I had to adjust to a new and sometimes quirky regime. My new mentor was able enough, especially on matters involving finance or figures, but there was no saying how a discussion with him would develop. Sometimes it proceeded reasonably to a satisfactory conclusion; but too often it became a monologue about some other problem of which he had been reminded, or other administrative battle in which he had been engaged. By this stage in my career I had no feelings, at least not many, about having my drafts amended. But I preferred not to have to sit beside the re-drafter as he wondered whether it might be better to say . . . or, no, perhaps we could . . . or, better still, how about . . .? This re-drafting of his own re-drafting I found very tiresome. There were, however, compensations. He could be very affable, and when he had made up his mind about the line to be followed, he could pursue it resolutely and effectively.

For eighteen months or so I performed the usual functions of an AP as in my housing days — drafting letters, preparing draft replies to PQs and ministerial correspondence, attending meetings and, if the most junior person present, drafting the minutes. I brought with me to the job no knowledge of the health service or its problems. I was at first almost completely ignorant about the administrative structure of the service and how it worked. This is of course a problem facing any civil servant entering a new job in a new field. Study of the Acts, the Statutory Instruments, the departmental circulars and some current files provided at least a basic background. Less easy to remedy by recourse to such formal documents was my ignorance of the general issues in the health field and in particular the organisation of medical work in hospitals.

Apart from a brief out-patient visit at an early age to have something simple done to my tonsils and adenoids, I had never been a hospital patient. None of my friends or relatives was a doctor; being young and healthy I had no particular interest in health and seldom read the health columns of the newspapers, less extensive then, I think, than in this neurotic age. Visits to hospitals to see friends or relatives had left me with only a thankfulness that I was able at the end of the visiting period to walk out through the door, and I had taken with me no desire to increase what ordinary observation had told me about how these forbidding institutions were run. Now in my first floor room (or to be accurate the room I shared with two higher executive officers) I became more aware of the extent of my ignorance on some matters which were basic in the context of my new job. What exactly was the difference between mental illness and mental deficiency, between a pathologist and a bacteriologist, between a consultant and a specialist, between the functions of the General Medical Council and the British Medical Association? On these and many other matters, I was enlightened by my boss, by my juniors and by the medical staff in the Department.

I was surprised to find after a few weeks how much, granted my initial ignorance, and, be it said, some aversion from health questions, I was enjoying work in this new field. I should not have been surprised, for I was dealing with general issues of policy far from the sight, sound and smell of hospital wards. Moreover, for an administrator, even a junior one, the interest and satisfaction derives to a considerable extent from the successful operation of the administrative machine whatever the field in which he is engaged. But there were other grounds for surprise. The political battles and policy debates about the introduction of the NHS were over. The issues with which I was dealing were narrow and detailed — gradings, pay and allowances — much narrower than the broad questions of social policy on the housing front, and much narrower than the kind of questions which had occupied my mind at the university. Then I had pontificated on the performance of Prime Ministers and commented on the rise and fall of Empires. Sometimes the transition was rather dispiriting when I became tangled in the complications of mileage allowances, whether another ha'penny a mile was justified. But this immersion in detail began to bring the satisfaction of really knowing about something which mattered to many people out there, and, as the weeks went on, of speaking with some knowledge and conviction in discussions with my boss and colleagues.

I was introduced to discussions of a more exalted kind — meetings between the Department, represented by the Under Secretary responsible for Health Services, the Chief Medical Officer, and sundry members of the medical and administrative hierarchies down to myself, and representatives of the hospital doctors. These discussions were more urbane and less rhetorical than those which I remembered with representatives of local authorities. This is not to say that the doctors were any more public-spirited or any less concerned to seek their own advantage (why not?). But the arguments were more elegantly put, and when the daggers were out they were wielded with more style and finesse. I was, of course, only an observer and note-taker; but I enjoyed these civilised encounters.

Before long there came an opportunity to graduate from my usual state of tutelage and perform a more responsible role. The legislation setting up the NHS in Scotland had provided for the establishment of a 'Scottish Health Services Council' and various specialist advisory committees. The Advisory Committee on Hospital and Specialist Services decided to set up a sub-committee to consider arrangements for the reception and welfare of hospital in-patients. A country gentleman who was chairman of a hospital board of management was appointed chairman; some of the members represented the various interested professional groups, medical, nursing and administrative; others were identified with no particular interest except that of the patient. I was appointed secretary. The job of secretary of such a committee, or of any Government committee appointed to study a specific issue, is not merely to write the minutes, but with the chairman to organise the work of the committee, to produce papers for them to consider, to write to interested bodies seeking views and information, and in due course to draft their report. All of this involves more independent action and initiative, albeit under the authority of the committee, than ordinary work at AP level in the Department.

This, too, I found congenial. The country gentleman was a decent old boy, not accustomed to a national role away from his home ground, and very glad to have suggestions and guidance. Only occasionally did he have inflexible views ('No, we can't have a meeting on that date; it's our point-to-point'). We had lively and sometimes entertaining meetings. A hospital matron reminded us of the implications for nurses of some of the more utopian ideas that floated round the table. The administrator doggedly kept costs in mind. One of the lay members was determined that we should emphasise the need to get bed-pans to patients as soon as they needed them (it was seldom indeed that a meeting passed without a passionate plea for bed-pans). The issues were not complicated, technical or controversial; there was broad agreement among members on what they wanted to say, and I did not find it difficult to draft the report.

Some of the recommendations in the report were obvious or even trite. Patients should be treated as individuals, not as cases; they should be given as much information as possible before coming into hospital and during their stay; when leaving they should be given full instructions and guidance about what they ought and ought not to do. Obvious, yes — but there were hospitals where patients were not being treated in this way. Waking times; arrangements for visitors; availability of sitting-rooms; circulation of books and magazines — these and other matters of importance to patients lying in bed or shuffling about the ward were explored and made the subject of practical recommendations. Hardly any of these recommendations, it is true, could not have been thought up by any sensible man or woman of goodwill and imagination. But there was some value in having them set out in one document, a document which was in due course accepted by the parent committee, and later the Secretary of State, and then printed and sent out under his authority to hospital boards for consideration and action. Members of boards and hospital staff who wanted to see improvements now had an official text and authority which they could pray in aid.

Sometime about the middle of 1951 my principal was promoted to assistant secretary and moved to take charge of another health service division of the Department. I was naturally interested to see what would happen now. In the ordinary course either an existing principal would be transferred from another branch or someone would be promoted. Might that someone be me? I was now 28, if only just, the age at which it seemed assistant principals performing well began to be considered for promotion. Or would certain events in my past be held against me?

I was told by the assistant secretary, Norman Graham, that the principal post would not be filled immediately. No reason was given. Meanwhile I was to carry on as if the principal was on holiday, doing what I could myself, and looking to him, the assistant secretary, for advice and support. This was quite encouraging; at least the door was not being closed by the appointment of A. N. Other. I was happy to act as if I was a principal, even if I was acting unpaid, in the hope that in a short time the Department would make an honest principal of me.

For the next few months I soldiered on. By the late autumn I was becoming a little restive. I was sitting in the principal's chair (literally), doing the work he had been doing, and there was no sign of any regularisation of the position. Towards the end of November just as I was thinking of raising the matter directly but delicately, I was summoned to the Secretary's room and told that as from the beginning of December I would be promoted and would continue to do my present job. I returned to my desk well content.

I remained at that desk until the autumn of 1957. The main elements of my responsibility remained the same — hospital medical staffing and ambulance services — but as life went on other subjects were assigned to me for longer or shorter periods. Seven years is a longer period of service than is normal in one principal post. The habit in the Civil Service is to move people about. There are no precise rules about this; but principals, in my day, might normally expect to be moved after four or five years to another job, perhaps in a completely different field. In the Department of Health, and I suppose in these days in the Ministry of Health, a principal having served for a while in a health service post might find himself in Town and Country Planning.

There are some advantages in this; people do not become stale in one job and can bring a fresh eye to a new job. But there are also disadvantages. Some knowledge of the field with which one is dealing is needed to be fully effective in an administrative job and this only comes with some experience on the job. This is, curiously, more true at the middle levels of a large organisation, where one deals with more detailed, almost technical, questions, than at senior levels where the issues are more general. And there are sometimes difficulties for outside bodies — professional organisations, hospital boards, trade associations — when their normal departmental contact is moved, and a new boy ignorant of their problems (or worse, who thinks he knows more than he does) moves in to his seat. On the whole the system works reasonably well provided changes of field are not too frequent.

I do not know whether after seven years in the job I had become stale. But by the end of that time it would have been surprising if I had not become something of an expert in my limited field, especially on the complexities of the pay terms and conditions of service for hospital medical and dental staff. By 1957 these covered many pages of small print.

Whitley Councils consisting of representatives of management and staff were responsible for negotiating the pay and conditions of service for the various groups of staff in the NHS. I was a member of the group known as Medical Committee B which dealt with hospital medical and dental staff. I had a hand in drafting the circulars to hospital boards setting out the results of these negotiations; and I corresponded with the boards on the one hand and the Scottish Office of the BMA on the other about doubts, difficulties and hard cases.

Responsibility for medical staffing during these seven years involved, however, not only the technicalities of conditions of service but many aspects, albeit administrative aspects, of doctors' work — the organisation of specialist services and their availability in various parts of the country; recruitment to the different specialities; the arrangements for a pre-registration year in hospitals for medical graduates; doctors' part in the administration of hospitals. For my education in these arcane matters I was much indebted to the medical staff of the Department. The relations between administrative and professional staffs in the Civil Service have often been the subject of comment and discussion; and I shall add to that later.

I was involved, too, in regular contact with my opposite numbers in the Ministry of Health. Although some aspects of NHS arrangements in Scotland were different from those in England (for example the Ambulance Service in

Scotland was run by a single national body while in England it was run by local authorities) the service on the ground in these two countries was on similar lines. On one important matter — the salaries and conditions of staff — the arrangements had to be identical. On NHS policy generally the two Health Departments had to keep in touch to ensure that they marched in step, or if they did not, it was by agreement and for good reason. On most matters of common interest, and especially on salaries and conditions of service, the Ministry as the larger Department with the larger responsibility took the lead. It was they who provided secretaries for the management sides of the various negotiating bodies; and it was they who sought Treasury agreement for additional expenditure.

I was very fortunate in my opposite numbers at the Ministry. There was first a philosophy graduate who sported a bow tie, a languid air and a very sharp mind. As secretary of the management side of Medical Committee B he would ring me up — or I would ring him up — and we would exchange ideas. He would send me, for comment, draft papers he had prepared; and when I was in London we would have lunch together in the Ministry canteen. He was succeeded by a charming lady who was equally co-operative. After one or two long days we even had dinner together (not in the canteen) before my departure for the night train. The management side consisted of representatives of the Health Departments and the hospital boards; the staff sides were composed of consultants in active practice, some of them extremely distinguished clinicians. Meetings were more an elegant ritual dance than a full-blooded discussion or debate. Each side knew the other's views, since the secretaries were in almost daily touch; but each spokesman would solemnly set out his side's position in some detail. Convention decreed that all the rest round the table, and there were over a dozen on each side, would normally preserve a discreet silence (an expensive silence if the hourly remuneration of those present was calculated). There would be some polite if sometimes slightly barbed exchanges after the initial statements had been made, and some kind of agreement, if only to study the matter further, would be reached. Normally, in practice, Medical Committee B settled only conditions of service. Ministers were unlikely to be interested in, say, mileage allowances for domiciliary visits; but they were very interested in pay and the repercussions of any increases. The big decisions about salaries were therefore usually made elsewhere with Medical Comittee B giving them its imprimatur.

I had other contacts with the Ministry. The number of aspects of NHS policy to be considered by the central administration was about the same in a relatively small Scotland as it was in a relatively large England and Wales. Because, however, of the size of its task in terms of the population, the number of institutions and the health service staff for which it was responsible, the Ministry had far more staff than we had. It followed that someone in DHS had more subjects to cover than someone of comparable grade in the Ministry, and therefore I and my DHS colleagues each had several opposite numbers in the Ministry. The energies of each of these Ministry officials were concentrated in a narrow field, and when general questions of policy arose on a matter in which England, Wales and Scotland were all concerned they normally made the running. I therefore found myself knocking on several different doors in the Ministry's offices in Savile Row and Russell Square.

Involvement with the Ambulance Service led me into a very different world from that of the pin-striped consultants. In Scotland, the Ambulance Service was provided by St. Andrew's Ambulance Association and the Scottish Branch of the Red Cross acting together. The cost was borne by the Secretary of State, and he had two representatives on the management committee which ran the service — my assistant secretary and myself. As the Department met the bills, we had a considerable say in the work of the committee, of which all the other members were representatives of the two voluntary bodies. The total mileage run by ambulances grew steadily year by year as the expectations of patients and doctors increased. We tried to keep the increase in mileage under reasonable control and from time to time sent out exhortations to general practitioners and to hospitals urging them to restrict the use of ambulances to cases of real medical need. But what was 'need'? There was no objective measure and we were in the doctors' hands. (A few of the doctors, we thought, but could not prove, were in the patients' hands.) As more out-patient clinics were opened, and as physiotherapy became increasingly available, the mileage inexorably increased.

In the main centres there were full-time ambulance staff, but in the country areas very often a local garage proprietor ran the ambulance on contract. When a call came, it sometimes resulted in a garage employee removing from his person the more obvious marks of his calling and driving off to pick up the patient. Sometimes he had to call upon a neighbour or a passer-by to lend a hand with the stretcher. Although in those days consumers and patients were less disposed to complain than they are now, these unsophisticated arrangements were far from satisfactory and brought criticism on the service. Over the years we managed to increase the number of full-time ambulance service employees and reduce the amount of single-manning of vehicles. But the nature of the population distribution in Scotland and the limitations on Exchequer finance made it impossible to ensure that two neatly uniformed men would appear with the ambulance in response to every call in the remoter rural areas.

The management committee had all the usual responsibilities of management — recruiting staff; providing and maintaining premises; analysing costs; selecting and purchasing equipment, particularly, in their case, new ambulances. There were negotiations with the unions about pay and conditions. But there was another dimension of management in this particular context of which my senior colleague and I had to take account. Although St. Andrew's and the Red Cross were partners in providing a national publicly-funded ambulance service, they continued their own activities in the first-aid and nursing fields as voluntary bodies. The most genuine dedication of voluntary organisations to good works does not necessarily exclude rivalry towards other organisations in the field; and we sometimes had to be honest brokers and peace-makers as well as managers.

By the mid-1950s most public services were involved in Civil Defence planning and preparations. The Scottish Home Department was responsible for the co-ordination of Civil Defence activity in Scotland, informing other departments about the assumptions on which they should plan the services for which they would be responsible in any future war. My branch in DHS was responsible for planning hospital and casualty services. (When I say here and elsewhere 'my branch was responsible' I am of course far from claiming sole responsibility. I was working under an assistant secretary with several branches in his division and an under secretary with several assistant secretaries under his wing. The medical staff were also deeply involved, and in this field were often the leading partners.) A nuclear bomb on a major city would destroy the hospitals and most of the inhabitants. But on the periphery of the blast there would be survivors; we had to consider how some kind of casualty service could be provided. Radiation would be, to put it at its lowest, an additional complication not encountered in earlier conflicts in Europe. Any sensitive spirit when first brought to contemplate the consequences of mass slaughter is bound to recoil in distaste. But it was not our business to wring our hands and lament or to consider whether the bomb should be banned; we had to make such provision, on paper at least, as imagination, prudence and common sense would suggest. And for most of us engaged in Civil Defence, in whatever field, it was, after the shock of the first immersion, just another job, or perhaps another aspect of our ordinary job, involving no more emotion or anguish, though more imagination, than, say, consideration of travelling expenses for members of hospital boards.

It did involve, however, some unusual forms of extra-mural activity. There were occasional visits to the Civil Defence Staff College in a splendid manor house at Sunningdale in Berkshire. From time to time exercises were arranged in specially prepared holes in the ground or even ordinary conference chambers in various parts of Scotland to test how in a nuclear war the different services — the warning organisation, police, fire, rescue, scientific advisers, casualty services, the army and other armed services — would be controlled or directed to where they would be most effective, and how some kind of government would be carried on. I did not personally find this playing at soldiers, necessary as it was, particularly congenial. More congenial — for reasons, it must be confessed, secondary if not irrelevant to the main object of the exercise — were the gatherings we arranged for doctors, nurses and health service staff at Taymouth Castle in Perthshire.

Taymouth Castle had for many years been the seat of the Marquesses of Breadalbane; in the 1930s it had found a new role as a rather grand country house hotel; during the war it had been a hospital for Polish servicemen; and in the 1950s it became a Civil Defence School. For most of the time its permanent staff ran courses for civil defence volunteers; but from time to time it was available to us in the Department to bring together people from hospital boards, the hospitals themselves and the ambulance services. We tried on them our ideas and our plans, and some kind of policy emerged which back at St. Andrew's House we had to set out in the usual departmental circulars.

These were residential gatherings. A valuable spin-off was that by the end of a few days people who had known each other only on an ordinary official basis now knew each other much better; and people who had known each other only as correspondents, or even as names, now knew each other as individuals. Apart from serious sessions about casualty collection — in grand salons where in years gone by the talk had been about casualties among the grouse population — we had walks in the grounds, some trout fishing in the Tay, and drinks at the bar. The Castle staff noted that the record for takings at the bar previously held by a husky group of rescue workers was beaten by our course for hospital matrons, who preferred gin, brandy and whisky to half-pints. If the results of burns, blast and radiation sickness began to depress the spirit, there was uplift to be found in gazing out of the windows at the glories of the Perthshire landscape or looking forward to a game of billiards with someone who had metamorphosed from difficult correspondent into congenial companion.

To provide additional manpower in time of war we organised a National Health Service Reserve of nursing and ambulance staff. St. Andrew's and the Red Cross had a major role in recuiting and training the volunteers. In the British way, these volunteers did not restrict themselves to the serious business in hand; they soon developed an impressive range of social activities. One function in Glasgow to which my wife and I were invited remains in my mind for the warmth if not the elegance of the greeting at the door, 'Mr Hume, Mrs Hume, wur awful glad yuv came!'

These extra-mural diversions were only occasional breaks from the conventional hard days at the office. One intra-mural activity was of such an unusual kind that it too was an interesting and educational diversion from the ordinary run of business.

It had been part of the basis on which hospital doctors entered the NHS that consultants would be eligible for 'distinction awards' in addition to salary to recognise that in private practice some consultants because of their particular skills or talents could charge higher fees than others. These awards were payable to about one third of consultants — 4% were given A awards, 10% B awards, and 20% C awards. The value of an A award was £2,500, almost as much as the maximum salary at that time for a full-timer; a B award brought £1,500 and a C award £500. Part-timers received the appropriate proportion of the award. (This awards system is still in being though there have been some changes, especially in the value of the awards.) To decide who should be paid awards the Government had set up a committee under Lord Moran, a retired consultant known best to the public as Winston Churchill's medical adviser. Apart from the vice-chairman, a retired senior administrative civil servant appointed no doubt to keep an eye on propriety and the public interest in what was certainly an unusual system for determining remuneration, all the members were distinguished consultants. These included three Scottish consultants and it was the practice for consultants in Scotland to be considered by a Scottish Sub-Committee consisting of these three plus three or four other senior consultants. Their recommendations then went to the main committee.

I acted as secretary of the Scottish Sub-committee, and with the three Scots on the main committee attended meetings of that body in London. Death, retirement and increases in the total number of consultants meant that new awards had to be made each year. Lord Moran's chairmanship was marvellous to behold. He sat hunched in his chair, his eyes darting round the table. Papers were spread before him but he seemed to know or know about every consultant in England whose time for consideration had come. He had been round the so-called Provinces with the vice-chairman, holding meetings with senior consultants, hearing views and taking notes. He reeled off comments on the consultants whose names appeared on the lists. For some there was unreserved commendation; the qualities of others were weighed in the balance. A was a good operator but his judgment was occasionally suspect; B was diligent in promoting research but could do more to reduce his waiting list; C was very helpful to general practitioners but was not as co-operative as he might be with consultant colleagues.

It was a bravura performance, self-confident, never at a loss for a word, showing no expectation of challenge. But sometimes challenge there was from a bold spirit at the other side of the table who would elegantly but firmly argue in favour of X or against Y. Lord Moran was sometimes convinced but not often. After all, he would remind his auditors, he had spent weeks going round England and Wales consulting everyone of note. There were some awkward moments when distinguished men refused to be bull-dozed. But Lord Moran had not got where he was by being easily persuaded, and more often than not his will prevailed. When unconvinced by the Chairman's flow of words and argument one eminent surgeon made no secret of his dissent, raising his eyes to heaven, or in extreme cases lifting his hands six inches from the table and letting them drop audibly. Only in one respect did Lord Moran invariably acknowledge the greater knowledge, if not the greater wisdom, of some members of his committee — he never challenged the recommendations of the Scottish Sub-Committee.

The atmosphere and the procedures at meetings of that body were different from those of the main committee. Individual members had undertaken local consultations; and the smaller size of the consultant body in Scotland, though larger in proportion to population that the comparable body in England and Wales, meant that individual consultants were more likely to be known to several members. While discussion was relaxed and informal, opinions were very carefully expressed. I enjoyed listening to well-rounded appraisal of performances, only occasionally suspecting that punctilious phraseology concealed strong personal feelings.

It became the custom for the Royal College of Surgeons of Edinburgh and the Royal College of Physicians of Edinburgh to alternate in giving us lunch on the occasion of our day-long annual meeting. I was never sure whether it was because of the different traditions of these two bodies or the different habits of their Presidents that we always had splendid food and wine at Surgeons' Hall and a rather plain unexciting repast at the Physicians' premises in Queen Street. There was always interesting table-talk. On one occasion a member of the Sub-Committee told me that only once, and it had been about thirty years before, had he told a man he was going to die. The man had not died; in due course he had made a good recovery, and the consultant had seen him walking along Princes Street only a week before our conversation. Whether magnificently or adequately refreshed, the Sub-Committee returned to their task apparently unaffected by the nature of the hospitality they had just enjoyed.

There have been attacks on the awards system from time to time, and perhaps as long as it lasts there will be periodic criticism of an arrangement under which large sums of public money are in effect disbursed by a group of consultants to some of their professional colleagues. But if some consultants are to be paid more than others — and if there were no NHS some consultants, like some architects, some opera singers and some barristers, would certainly be paid more than others — who is likely to be better able to distribute awards than other consultants, so senior and distinguished as to be above the battle? No doubt some 'errors' will be made; but in the following year and the year after that, there will be another chance for those not selected, and as the years go by the selectors change and move on. In any selection process, whether for promotion in a hierarchical organisation or for inclusion in a football team, there are liable to be differences of view both among the choosers and those who observe the results of their choosing. It is perhaps an indication that it is not too bad an arrangement that the awards system has lasted so long in a world where change is endemic.

All these matters which concerned me in the early and mid-fifties were far from the major dramas of politics. True, there were Parliamentary Questions and ministerial correspondence — about, for example, the inadequacy of the ambulance service at X, or the need for more consultant orthopaedic surgeons at Y. When these arrived on my desk I made the necessary enquiries of the Ambulance Service or the hospital board, perhaps putting a little pressure on them if this seemed justified (but always bearing in mind the needs of other areas about whom no one happened to be asking Questions). Then draft replies were put forward defending what could properly be defended, acknowledging shortcomings which could not, indicating when improvements could be expected or, if that were not possible, accepting the need for better services as resources became available. I do not recall any personal encounters with ministers who were at the receiving end of these papers. Such ministerial interest as there was in the general policy about use of ambulances or increases in the number of consultants involved my senior officers, not me.

I did not feel deprived because of this. I enjoyed my job and worked with agreeable colleagues. The staff of my branch consisted of a higher executive officer, an executive officer, a clerical officer and a clerical assistant. They collected statistical information about medical and dental staff in hospitals and use of ambulances and produced various tables for general use: they provided me or anyone else who needed it with information as required; they prepared at my request drafts of letters, including sometimes ministerial correspondence; and they dealt direct with hospital boards and the Ambulance Service on routine matters, consulting me as necessary.

By 1954 I must have been accepted as a suitable person to introduce new assistant principals to the work of the Department. In that year there was posted to my branch for training a young lady straight from Newnham College, Cambridge; and the following year when she moved elsewhere, she was followed by another young lady from Lady Margaret Hall, Oxford. Both had been at school in England though the second was of Scottish parentage. (This sample of two was not representative of the kind of people entering the Scottish Office as assistant principals. Most were male, Scottish and educated at Scottish schools and universities.) I gave them the kind of jobs I was given in my early days, and they both did very well.

Apart from the daily administrative round, I was able to observe and participate in the tribal customs, changing and unchanging, of the Department. On the first working day after the New Year, it had long been the practice, following old Scottish custom, for the Secretary to go round the whole office shaking hands with each member of staff and offering best wishes for the New Year. For whatever reason, personal reluctance on someone's part, pressure of work, fading interest in such old-world traditions, or simply because there were fewer staff about as more of them added part of their annual leave entitlement to the regular New Year holiday, this habit stopped in the 1950s.

The annual office dance — black (or even white) ties and long frocks — continued to be a great occasion in the splendid Assembly Rooms in George Street. Tuneful, rhythmic and not too loud music of the twenties, thirties and forties was played by a seven or eight piece dance orchestra. It was on one such occasion when, during the band's interval, I was doing my best to emulate Fats Waller and Charlie Kunz at the piano, that a senior officer told me I could make more money doing that than I was likely to make as a civil servant. I was not quite sure what message he wanted to convey. But it was not to be long before the cult of informality and the desire for more decibels would sweep that civilised gathering away.

Golf, a game for some, an obsession for others, continued unabated. The office golf club had regular outings to courses round Edinburgh. Even Muirfield, always careful to preserve its special standing, seemed happy to welcome a large gathering of assorted bureaucrats from clerical assistants to Secretary. The most obsessional of all on such occasions was Douglas Haddow, under secretary in charge of health services, later to be Permanent Under Secretary of State for Scotland. Attired, according to the weather, either in plus fours or in shorts, he would play two or sometimes three rounds of almost immaculate golf pausing only to take sustenance and to exhort and sometimes berate the weaker brethren.

Other interests and obsessions found outlet in the horticultural society. Once a year the canteen, the venue for the annual show of flowers, vegetables and home baking, was awash with dahlias, sprays of sweet peas, larger than life onions and platefuls of scones and gingerbread.

There were less happy occasions when many of us made our way to crematorium, church or cemetery to bid farewell to a departed colleague or a former colleague whose retirement had come to an end. We seemed most often to be at the crematorium. We would stand outside waiting for the hearse to arrive. We followed the relatives inside; opened the hymn book, very often at the well-thumbed page on which the 23rd Psalm appeared; listened to words recalling not only our colleague but a loved husband, father, aunt or sister whom others had known much better than we had; shook hands as we went out with the near relatives, distressed or composed; and returned to the files on our desks.

All this time my working days were spent in the same room looking south across the city, another principal sharing it with me. My room-mate changed once or twice during this period. With only one — the one who remained longest — did I fail to develop a close relationship.

He was a man about fifteen years older than I who had joined the Civil Service during the war. He was very deaf and, no doubt partly because of this, very withdrawn. Even after two or three years it was seldom, in spite of some effort on my part, that our morning salutation went beyond 'Good Morning'. He would sometimes appear wet and bedraggled after having been caught in the rain while walking from his house deep in the country to the village where he boarded a bus for the city. On these occasions he would change his shoes and socks, hanging the damp hosiery over the radiator to dry. Often he carried a haversack which he hung up on the coat rack. What it contained I seldom knew. One day when he was absent from the room I was puzzled by strange squeaking noises. I checked door and windows, and just when I had identified the haversack as the source of the mystery, someone whom I had never seen before entered the room, lifted two very lively kittens from the haversack and departed. Another day my room-mate bore with him into the room even more threatening impedimenta — a large bow and stock of arrows. It was only then that I learned he was a member of the Royal Company of Archers, the Queen's Bodyguard in Scotland. As membership of this body is as much an indication of social distinction as of skill in archery, he must have been, as they say, well-connected.

I often suspected that, well-connected or not, he had behind that impassive exterior human qualities and depths of character which I would have respected. But I was not alone in finding it difficult to break through his reserve. In the canteen at lunch time with chatter all around he would sit alone with a book before him, using one hand to manage his food and the other to help keep the book open at his page.

The variety of human character in the Civil Service is greater than the public, accustomed to newspaper stereotypes, probably realises. It is far from being a homogeneous mass of grey conformist men and women. I would think that it is more tolerant of idiosyncrasies than most sections of industry or commerce. My colleague, although he often seemed strange to the rest of us, made an honourable contribution to the work of the Department. When eventually he retired he entered training for the ministry of the Anglican Church.

It was a pity I hardly knew him.

Chapter 5

Royal Commission On Doctors' and Dentists' Pay

When I returned to the office after the New Year break at the beginning of 1957, I was asked to go and see the Establishment Officer. He told me that sometime in the spring I would be moved to London to occupy the principal post in charge of the Department's small liaison office in Dover House, Whitehall, for a period unspecified but not less than two years. The experience in London would be a valuable step in my career.

This brought no joy to my heart. The London job involved keeping in touch generally with the Ministry of Health and other London departments and attending inter-departmental meetings when our Department's interest did not require the attendance of the experts from Edinburgh. This, it seemed to me, meant that the incumbent was part messenger, part interpreter, part spokesman — not a derisory role, except that he exercised these functions only in relation to less important business. For matters of any real significance for the Department those directly responsible climbed aboard the night sleeper from Edinburgh. Apart from this, although I was happy to visit London from time to time, I had no wish to live there. To anyone of discernment accustomed to Edinburgh, the general quality of life in the south-east of England seemed deficient. No promotion was involved in this transfer, and when I asked about my prospects on my return I was told there could be no guarantee.

The interview terminated by my saying that I would think the matter over, and by my senior colleague indicating quietly but firmly that whatever emerged from my further thought the matter was decided.

Further consideration suggested to me that if the job was a valuable step in a principal's career there was a case for so organising the period of tenure that most principals, or the younger ones at least, could benefit. Why, since the job involved no building up of expertise in a specific field, could the appointment not be for one year instead of 'at least two'? When I put this idea to the Establishment Officer it was received coolly. The atmosphere became even cooler when I said I would raise the matter with the FDA (the First Division Association, the staff association for members of the Administrative Class). My FDA colleagues agreed that to the extent that the job was valuable to the occupant it should be shared around; and to the extent that for Edinburgh people it was a hard lying job, the pain, also, should be shared. Representations on these lines were made by the FDA, and in the event the departmental hierarchy agreed that the London appointment should be for one year only. It was apparent, however, that my efforts to change the departmental mind were not highly regarded in some quarters.

Meantime, a much more important drama was unfolding. In June 1956, the British Medical Association had submitted to the Government a claim for an increase of not less than 24% in doctors' remuneration to take account of the fall in the value of money since 1951. A few weeks later the doctors were informed that the Government did not accept the premises on which the claim was based and did not feel justified in considering any claim for a general increase in the circumstances of the time. This rather lofty brush-off resulted in further exchanges about the basis on which the doctors had joined the NHS in 1948, and whether there had been any contract or undertaking to keep their earnings in line with increases in the cost of living and earnings in other professions. In an increasingly hostile atmosphere the Government denied the existence of any such obligations; they also made it clear that they had expressed no opinion on the merits of the claim. In their view economic circumstances made it impossible to consider the claim at that time.

To the ordinary worker, whether a white-coated doctor or a boiler-suited mechanic, there is not much difference between a decision not to consider a claim and a decision to reject it. The doctors were incensed. It looked as if a major confrontation (as it would now be called) between the profession and the Government was inevitable. Dentists too were in dispute about pay. Perhaps the NHS itself was in danger. Drawing back from the brink early in the New Year the Government decided that it would be prudent not merely to refer these disputes to an independent body, but to ask that body to look thoroughly at how doctors' and dentists' pay should be determined and how it should be kept under review. In February the Prime Minister announced that a Royal

Commission would be set up. Its full terms of reference as set out in the Royal Warrant dated 27th March were:

To consider

(a) How the levels of professional remuneration from all sources now received by doctors and dentists taking part in any part of the National Health Service compare with remuneration received by members of other professions, by other members of the medical and dental professions and by people engaged in connected occupations:

(b) What in the light of the foregoing should be the proper current levels of remuneration of such doctors by the National Health Service:

(c) Whether, and if so what, arrangements should be made to keep that remuneration under review:

And to make recommendations.

Sir Harry Pilkington was appointed Chairman and eight other 'trusty and well beloved' persons were appointed to join him as 'Our Commissioners'.

Although I was concerned with the pay of hospital doctors and hospital dentists, the recent exchanges with the profession had taken place at exalted levels and had not involved me directly. Quite suddenly, I was brought on to the stage, albeit in a modest supporting role. I was told that the Ministry of Health was to provide a full-time secretary for the Commission, and I was to act as a part-time secretary combining this with my new departmental job in Dover House.

It is an interesting comment on British administration that even when the appointment of a Royal Commission or other Government-appointed committee is the result of a dispute or policy disagreement in which the Government has been a party, no one seems to find it objectionable that the secretary should be a civil servant and should come from a department involved in the dispute. It may be a tribute to civil servants' capacity to work wholly in the interests of their masters of the moment. In my case, as I was to work at the same time for both the Department and the Commission, it implied the possibility of erecting Chinese walls, before these were invented by the stockbroking classes and the press. I was delighted; during my period in London I would have at least one continuing job of real substance and interest. By chance, Sir Harry Pilkington was to be in Edinburgh on other business in a few days time, and a message arrived saying he would call to see me. I knew he was Chairman of Pilkington Brothers, the major glass manufacturer; *Who's Who* told me he had recently been the President of the Federation of British Industries, and was a current director of the Bank of England.

Who's Who, with its cool biographical data, had not prepared me for the energy and exuberance which filled the room when Sir Harry Pilkington bounded in a few days later and grasped me by the hand. He was glad we would be working together on this important task. Not that he knew much about it; but that, he supposed, was one of the qualifications for the job. He went on to tell me about his meeting at No. 10 Downing Street when the Prime Minister had asked him to be Chairman. The policeman guarding the door had seemed slightly surprised when he arrived on his bicycle and proceeded to park it against the railings. There was no point in having a car in central London, Sir Harry told me. You could get from A to B much more quickly on your bike, and it was also much easier to park. Saying he would arrange a meeting of the Commission at his London office as soon as possible, he breezed out as quickly as he had breezed in.

Selwyn House in a quiet elegant corner of St James's was both office and dwelling place for Sir Harry Pilkington when in London. Members of the Commission met each other and the secretaries for the first time one evening in the sitting room of his flat at the top of the building. Sir Harry went round dispensing drinks and badinage. Of the eight members, I had previously encountered only two, both of whom coincidentally bore the name 'Watson'. Some years before, I had met Sir Hugh Watson, a leading Edinburgh solicitor, whose daughter had been a fellow student of mine at the University. Along with several million others I had seen on television Mr Sam Watson, the Durham miners' leader. W. A. Fuller of the Ministry of Health had been appointed Secretary.

As members moved to and fro the chat kept returning to the job they had so innocently undertaken. The terms of reference implied a thorough examination of the pay of lots of people apart from doctors and dentists. That would take time. Perhaps even a year, someone said. Was Mr Sam Watson's tongue in his cheek when he suggested that however long it took we might find ourselves splitting the difference between the professions and the government?

Next morning the first meeting of the Royal Commission took place in the conference room on the ground floor of Selwyn House. Two features of that room were not easily forgotten. First, there was a splendid view west across the Green Park, an idyllic prospect untouched by sight or sound of traffic. Second, the large table around which we sat was made entirely of glass. There was at first a certain reluctance to put papers and then elbows on its hardly visible surface, but then, seeing Sir Harry drop his briefcase unceremoniously upon it, we put our faith in Pilkington's glass and did likewise.

When a group of people hitherto unknown to each other begin to consider a complex issue of which they have had no direct experience there is bound to be some confusion, mixed indeed with some over-simplification, as they cast about wondering where to begin. Sir Harry showed that behind the brisk bonhomie there was a shrewd and calculating mind. He soon had members focusing on the issues which had to be faced right away.

The medical and dental professions were very suspicious about the appointment of the Commission. Was it merely a ploy by the Government to get medical and dental pay off the agenda for an indefinite period? Were the terms of reference sufficiently wide to cover all the matters which the doctors and dentists considered relevant? Because of this and other concerns there was some danger that the professions might not cooperate with the Commission, and this would make its task all the more difficult. Members of the Commission agreed with the Chairman that he should make informal approaches to the leaders of the professions to establish at the outset some kind of working relationship.

There were two other practical matters to be dealt with. The Commission would have to find premises of its own — rooms for meetings, and offices for the staff. Sir Harry and the secretaries would pursue this with the Ministry of Works. And in order to give members of the Commission a detailed picture of the whole complex structure of doctors' and dentists' pay — without such a factual basis to start from the Commission would merely flounder about — the Health Departments would be asked to submit a Factual Memorandum. Views and arguments would be sought later.

And so the Royal Commission was launched. Within a week or two informal talks with professional leaders had established a *modus vivendi*, and the Commission issued a public statement explaining how it proposed to set about its task and the factors of which it would take account. This seemed to make the doctors and dentists happier and their cooperation seemed assured. Discussions with the Ministry of Works produced some offers which were not acceptable and then one which was — part of a magnificent house at 10 Carlton House Terrace next to the Duke of York Steps. The Health Departments, with long experience of Commissions and Committees and their needs, had started the preparation of a Factual Memorandum before the ink was dry on the Queen's signature on the Royal Warrant. Soon members of the Commission were spending long hours studying its dauntingly detailed text and tables.

The Commission was enjoined to compare doctors' and dentists' remuneration 'with the remuneration received by members of other professions'. It became evident very quickly that there was practically no published information about the remuneration of other professions apart from those — an untypical group — who were in some form of public employment. Detailed figures had to be found somehow. How about the Inland Revenue? They must have masses of information submitted by taxpayers. Their published material about the incomes of 'professional persons' (undifferentiated) was too broad. If they could be persuaded to break it down and give information at least by profession the Commission would be on its way. At meetings with officials from the Revenue the Commission received expressions of sympathy and offers of all possible help — except the detailed kind of information they were seeking. Information was given by taxpayers in confidence, said the Revenue, and it would be a breach of that confidence to use the information or reassemble in such a way that it could identify the earnings of individual professional groups such as solicitors or architects.

The Commission decided that it would have to do a major survey of its own, obtaining direct from a properly structured statistical example of members of each profession information about individuals' remuneration. This was unlikely to elicit the response required unless the professional associations commended it to their members. There began a round of meetings with leaders of the professions. Sir Harry, supported on each occasion by one or two members of the Commission and the secretaries, explained, persuaded and occasionally cajoled — and succeeded in obtaining support for the survey. Then began the detailed work of drafting questionnaires — a different one for each profession — and deciding how to obtain representative samples. Much of this fell upon the secretariat. We were joined by a statistician from the Government Social Survey who had experience of this kind of exercise in other fields. Even the uninstructed among members and secretaries became familiar with 'stratified samples' and other hitherto arcane statistical concepts. Drafts of questionnaires and methods of obtaining samples were discussed with each professional body in turn. It was only after more than seventy drafts had been prepared, dissected and amended that finality was reached on the battery of questions designed to give information not only about remuneration from all sources, but also about additional benefits on the one hand and expenses on the other. In one or two cases professional bodies, completely converted to the value of the survey, added some questions for their own purposes.

At the same time as we were in this way preparing to find the facts about what professional people were paid, we started a parallel exercise to obtain the views of the medical, dental and other professional organisations on all aspects of work in the professions concerned. Lists of questions had to be drawn up covering such matters as recruitment, security of employment, mobility and mortality, hours of work, liability to be on call, arrangements for retiral and superannuation, how remuneration was fixed and many others. Again the organisations had to be consulted. The views resulting from these enquiries would be set against the hard facts about actual pay resulting from the sampling surveys.

Lest it be thought that comparisons limited to professions strictly interpreted would be inadequate, twenty of the largest firms in the country and one nationalised industry were persuaded to supply information about the remuneration of graduates in their employment. All this work of preparing and launching these major enquiries took time — well over a year. The first questionnaires to doctors were sent out at the end of 1957 but it was almost the end of 1958 before the last of the questionnaires went out to other professions.

During most of this period, in fact until July 1958, I shuttled between 10 Carlton House Terrace, where I was part time assistant secretary to the Royal Commission, and Dover House in Whitehall, where for the other part of my time I was in charge of the London office of the DHS. My wife and I were living in a flat in a pleasant leafy part of Surrey between Walton-on-Thames and Weybridge. Each morning I arrived with hordes of other commuters at Waterloo Station and, inspired by lively martial music from the loudspeakers, walked smartly across Hungerford Bridge and installed myself in Dover House. Subject to what was happening, I normally stayed there until mid-morning, worked at Carlton House Terrace until about 4.00 p.m. and rounded off the day back at Dover House. But the Royal Commission had priority, and there were many days when I paid only the briefest of calls at Dover House, where I had excellent supporting staff.

This was a very enjoyable part of my official career. Although officially only part time, I attended all meetings of the Commission and took part in most of the discussions with professional bodies about the drafting of the questionnaires. Members of the Commission welcomed full participation of the secretaries in that kind of detailed discussion. It was interesting to see the leaders and senior officials of the professions in action — some grave, some voluble, some pompous, some unassuming, some laconic, some charming, some extroverted — all ultimately pledging help and cooperation. There was the intellectual challenge of devising questionnaires which would fit the circumstances of the different professions and produce information which would be reliable and comparable with that for other professions.

I have never been one of those earnest souls who seem oblivious to, or at least not much interested in, their surroundings. I enjoyed my second floor room looking south from Carlton House Terrace across St. James's Park — surely one of the best outlooks in London. While the window in my room in Dover House offered only a prospect of roof tops and chimneys, the building itself had a certain fascination. Built in the eighteenth century as the town house for a wealthy nobleman, it had housed in its time the French ambassador, Lady Caroline Lamb, who conducted a tempestuous affair with Lord Byron within its walls, and Lord Dover, who gave the house its present name (He is even more to be honoured for the benefaction which gave us the National Gallery.) Vacant in the 1880s, it was considered as a possible alternative to 10 Downing Street as a residence and office for the Prime Minister, but Mr Gladstone declined it, as he thought it too grand. What was too grand for one Prime Minister became his successor, Lord Salisbury's, choice as a base for the Secretary for Scotland, when that office was established in 1885. One can, however, see what Mr Gladstone meant. He was accustomed as Prime Minister to a modest terrace house constructed by an eighteenth century speculative builder. The principal rooms in Dover House are truly magnificent, their spacious interiors matched by splendid views across Horse Guards Parade to the Park. In the 1950s, and still today, these rooms were occupied by the Secretary of State, his ministerial colleagues and the Permanent Under Secretary of State. Lesser fry, which included heads of the four Scottish departments and other senior staff from Edinburgh on London visits, squeezed themselves into a curious collection of apartments and attics designed for occupation by footmen, cooks and housemaids. The back stairs by which most of these rooms were reached were very steep, and there was no lift. As I toiled up to my attic room carrying only my brief-case, I often thought of long-dead servant lasses bent under the weight of buckets of coal.

The route I had to take on my daily shuttle could not have been more agreeable. A few yards along Whitehall was Horse Guards, and even in those days before the boom in tourism began to endanger civilised life in capital cities, there were crowds of sightseers waiting to see the changing of the guard at 11.00 a.m. In summer the press was so thick that passage through the archway leading to Horse Guards Parade was difficult, and I had to change the time of my peregrination. Once I reached the Parade, historic official London lay all around — the back of 10 Downing Street on the left, the Admiralty on the right, and nearby the fortified bunker from which armies and navies had been controlled during the war. Across the Mall I went, with a leftwards glance along that fine processional way to Buckingham Palace in the distance. Then up the Duke of York Steps, and into No. 10 Carlton House Terrace. The human scene was interesting too — from the tourists of varied hue and costume to the conventional gentlemen in bowler hats and pin-stripe suits. One morning I saw a forlorn looking young lady dressed in dowdy old-fashioned clothes sitting on a suitcase halfway up the Duke of York Steps. She seemed very out of place and I looked closely as I passed by. Did I not know that face? I certainly did: it was Ingrid Bergman. And then I saw at the top of the steps, casually if not so dowdily dressed men and women standing expectant, with cameras and other equipment at the ready. A moment or two later as a troop of Horse Guards came into sight in the Mall at the foot of the steps, cameras began to roll, and a few seconds of *The Inn of the Sixth Happiness* with Ingrid Bergman watching horse and riders passing by was on film.

By mid-summer 1958 it was clear that the Commission still had a great deal of work ahead of it. Analysis of the results of the sampling enquiries would be a major exercise, and there would have to be meetings, some in public, with many of the organisations submitting written evidence, to probe and elucidate. The Chairman told me he would be glad if I could serve full time with the Commission when my year at Dover House came to an end, and on this new basis I would be made Joint Secretary. I was more than happy to do this, and the Department readily agreed.

The Commission decided that much of the detailed examination of the masses of information and evidence now flooding in should be done by small committees or *ad hoc* groups. One of these committees was to consist of the three members based in the north — Sir Hugh Watson, Mr Sam Watson and Mr I. D. McIntosh, headmaster of Fettes College — and it would be convenient to them to meet in Edinburgh with me as secretary.

And so it turned out that my wife and I ended what had been an enjoyable sojourn in Surrey and for the rest of the Commission's life my home base was once again in Edinburgh. There I usually spent the first two days of the week; I had a desk in a back room in St. Andrew's House, but found myself often with the members of the northern committee in Sir Hugh Watson's office in St. Andrew Square. Most Tuesday evenings saw me on the night train for London.

Meetings of other committees of the Commission itself normally took place in the latter part of the week, allowing Sir Harry and the other members to earmark at least part of the working week — apart from the evenings — for the service of those bodies which were the source of their own remuneration. I spent the nights of Wednesday and Thursday in the Caledonian Club just off Belgrave Square. I enjoyed my morning walk down Constitution Hill and along by the lake in St. James's Park to the Commission office. Depending on the business on Friday, I would either catch the late afternoon train to Edinburgh or wait for the night sleeper.

During the winter of 1958–59 the work went steadily on. As the results of the sampling surveys came in they were set out in voluminous tables showing the earnings of each profession under all kinds of heads — age, sex, type of work (e.g. consultants, general practitioners) and many others. Small groups, consisting sometimes only of the Chairman, the secretaries and the statistician from Social Survey, went over them in detail, comparing this figure with that, asking for a further analysis here and further comparison there, and deciding what were the significant points for inclusion in summaries for other members. It was absorbing work, the rest of us trying to be as sharp as the Chairman in seeing significant relationships and revealing differences.

If one single figure had to be chosen to compare earnings in different professions it might be the median earnings of those in the 30–60 age group. (The median is the figure above which are 50% and below which are 50% of the group.) We found that on this basis consultants had by far the highest; general practitioners came next followed by actuaries, and architects were lowest. But the median figures did not show the extent to which, in some professions more than others, there was a wide spread of incomes with a group of very high earners at the top.

When we compared the highest deciles (the figure of income above which there was 10% of the profession concerned) we found that the lead was taken by barristers, actuaries and consultants in that order. In some professions, it was possible on the other hand to earn a high income at an early age. In dentistry, where payment was by piece work, energetic young men and women under thirty could make more money than in any other profession, but they tailed off as age and perhaps other priorities took their toll. All things considered, the Commission thought the most useful single figure to compare one profession with another was the total of career earnings in the age group 30–65: that is, what the average practitioner might be expected to earn between these ages if the circumstances of 1955 (the year to which the survey related) remained unchanged. On this basis the league table was as follows:

	£
Consultants	117,000
Actuaries	105,000
Barristers	92,000
Solicitors (England and Wales)	88,000
Graduates in Industry	84,000
General Medical Practitioners	79,000
General Dental Practitioners	79,000
Advocates	72,000
Accountants	71,000
Solicitors (Scotland)	67,000
Surveyors	63,000
University Teachers	63,000
Engineers	59,000
Architects	54,000

Absorbing in a different way were the public sessions at which the Commission interviewed representatives of organisations which had sent in memoranda giving views and information (always known, curiously, in the jargon of committees as 'evidence'). The secretaries, having earlier gone over these memoranda with the appropriate committee of the Commission and prepared lists of possible questions, had a largely passive role listening to the chairman of the committee leading the questioning. Verbatim notes were taken by specially qualified shorthand writers. The leaders of the doctors and dentists were, naturally enough, concerned to bring out, and indeed make the most of, the difficulties and problems of medical and dental practice, thus demonstrating the need for compensating financial reward. It was the job of the Commission to get these arguments into perspective and occasionally to puncture the high flown rhetoric. Other professions, too, sought to demonstrate that their lot was not always a happy one. By the time we had had thirty such presentations of oral evidence supplementing written memoranda we thought we had a fairly full picture of professional activity in the United Kingdom.

By this time I had had considerable experience of working with members of the Commission, and knew or thought I did their individual strengths and characteristics. The star performer was certainly the Chairman. With all his love of banter and sometimes schoolboy humour he left no doubt who made the running and who was in charge. Nor was there any doubt, when difficult issues arose, that behind all the badinage a careful mind was at work which was never rushed into hasty decisions. He would not perhaps have been the best man to chair a Commission on some sensitive issue of social policy, but he was completely at home with figures and saw the reality behind them without being lost in detail. I never heard him utter a harsh word to anyone. The nearest he came to giving me a ticking-off was when I sent a letter to someone whose name, I had not noticed, was wrongly spelt. 'People are usually very sensitive about their names,' he said when pointing out my error.

It is perhaps inevitable that I should remember examples of his idiosyncratic behaviour rather than his contributions to an understanding of the figures. Once in spring he had me meet him at Euston Station in order to help him transport to No. 10 Carlton House Terrace a supply of daffodils from his garden at St. Helens when the Commission office looked so bleak. We carried armfuls to and from taxis and then distributed the golden sunshine round the office. One summer day when he expected a long meeting of the Commission he brought from Selwyn House a stock of ice for cooling drinks before lunch. When everyone was served and there was ice to spare his high spirits took over. Could anyone throw ice cubes as far as the Mall? No one volunteered to try and so he himself began flinging ice out of the open window. Most of it landed on the projecting roof of the basement below, but some seemed likely to endanger life on the pavement beyond. To the alarmed protests of his colleagues he replied, 'It's all right. If anyone is killed it will be the perfect murder. In less than two minutes there will be no sign of the murder weapon.' Fortunately, there were no anguished shouts and no bodies fell to the ground. Much relieved, we went to lunch.

Rivalling the Chairman in their penetration and understanding of the statistical data and the evidence presented were two other members: Mr J. H. Gunlake, a consultant actuary, and Professor John Jewkes, Professor of Economic Organisation at Oxford. As well as being professionally skilled in handling and interpreting statistics, Gunlake was very careful and precise in his exposition both of facts and arguments. It was sometimes difficult to live up to his high standards. He told us that it took him about half an hour to consider each foolscap page of an important draft. Jewkes was more interested in general policy. He was a right-wing economist opposed in general to state activity in the economic field, and therefore tended to be suspicious of Government departments in their dealings with professions employed in a publicly financed health service. He relentlessly pursued the arguments and closely analysed the premises on which they were based. As the months went by, it became apparent that he was taking a different view of the evidence from the rest of his colleagues. (And, incidentally, as the number of overnight stays in his London club increased, he told me that its library contained the largest collection of books of which he had read the first hundred or so pages.)

Not far behind the chairman and these two there was another group of members — Sir Hugh Watson, Sir David Hughes Parry, Professor of English Law at London University and Mr A. D. Bonham Carter, a director of Unilever — each quite different in personal style, who made a solid contribution to the Commission's work, probing, questioning and criticising. Sir Hugh was a stickler for the correct use of English. When someone used the word 'anticipate' when clearly 'expect' was meant, he urged us all to remember the difference between the lady who expected to be married and her friend who anticipated matrimony. Sir David in his lilting Welsh voice would steadily and almost diffidently question and further question those giving evidence, seldom betraying what he thought of the response he got. Bonham Carter, bluff, extroverted, was adept in Commission discussions at adding an incisive practical comment to someone else's delicately structured argument. If the remaining three members — Mrs K. Baxter, Mr Sam Watson and Mr McIntosh — did not play such a lively part in detailed discussion, each of them brought to the consideration of the main issues, good general judgement based on experience in other fields.

While all the data about earnings in the medical, dental and other fields had been flowing in, certain fundamental questions had never been far from Commissioners' minds — what factors should in fact determine levels of pay; what weight should be given to them; in the real world do differences in pay in fact reflect them? The evidence submitted had suggested various factors of which account should be taken — particularly the more demanding and less agreeable features of professional practice. In early 1959, as the Commissioners began to consider what might be their recommendations about medical and dental pay, they were aware that they had to reach a view on this question — a question which had for many years, indeed centuries, been debated in many quarters, from economists on the one hand to ordinary wage earners on the other, without any consensus emerging. The Commission drew up a list of no fewer than fourteen factors which, it could be argued, should have a bearing on remuneration — the nature of the qualifications for entry, length and cost of training, intelligence and other qualities required, differences in the nature of the work and responsibility, and ten others. But how to evaluate and give a precise weight to each of them? The Commission concluded that the relationship between earnings in different professions is determined not only by considerations of precise justice and logic, but also by tradition and economic pressures of various kinds. They decided to bear the fourteen factors in mind generally, but not to evaluate them in any precise sense.

The framing of the recommendations took many hours of discussion over many weeks. Finally, eight out of nine Commissioners agreed on new salary scales for each of the grades of hospital medical and dental staff, new figures for distinction awards, and new average earnings for general medical practitioners on the one hand and general dental practitioners on the other. Professor Jewkes considered the proposed new earnings should be higher, and decided to set out his own proposals in a memorandum of dissent. While comparison of the Commission's proposals with the claims of the professions showed different relationships in relation to different groups, their overall effect was to suggest lower increases than those for which the professions had argued. On the other hand, while the Government had not themselves suggested specific figures, the increases suggested by the Commission were almost certainly higher than they would have wished.

Important as it was to recommend new levels of pay, the Commission thought it just as important, perhaps more important, to devise, in response to the last part of their terms of reference, new arrangements for keeping pay under review so that dangerous disputes would be avoided in the future. They considered various possibilities — direct negotiation; arbitration; the use of some kind of automatic adjusting formula. Each of them was considered unsatisfactory in the circumstances of the professions. In the event, they decided to recommend the appointment by the Government after consultation with the professions of a Standing Review Body composed of people of experience in various fields of national life to keep the remuneration of the doctors and dentists under review and to make recommendations about remuneration to the Prime Minister. The Commission recognised that such a body would be advisory only, that the Government would be free to reject its recommendations, and that this would not give the professions an absolute assurance that this remuneration would not be determined by political convenience. But they did not think it reasonable to suggest that the Government should be asked to abrogate its functions completely in a matter of this kind; and they believed that seven people such as they had in mind would make recommendations of such weight and authority that the Government would be able, and indeed would feel bound, to accept them.

It was for the Commissioners themselves to decide what recommendations they wanted to make; and they did. In the discussions about the recommendations, interventions by the secretaries were limited to detailed, almost technical, comments about the implications of, say, extending the length of an incremental scale or narrowing the gap between one grade and another. After all, the Commission was as much concerned with administrative detail as with broad policy. Their recommendations would in due course be picked over by experts on pay and conditions, professional negotiators and quite possibly ill-disposed persons with a talent for destructive criticism. It was important that the recommendations should hang together and be consistent, from the amount of the proposed new top distinction award for consultants to the provision for dentists in remote areas. And so comments by the secretaries on detailed implications were seldom unwelcome.

Fuller and I did, however, play a major role in drafting the report. We submitted to the Commission a skeleton outline suggesting chapter headings and contents. When a final version of this was agreed, we divided between us responsibility for preparing first drafts of each of the chapters. Apart from presenting the Commission's recommendations in full and the reasons behind them, the report had first of all to set out a brief history of doctors' and dentists' pay, a good deal of factual material about the current pay structures, a full account of the sampling enquiries about professional remuneration and the results (illustrating these with many tables). Then came the Commission's thoughts on the implications of all that for doctors and dentists. Drafts were circulated to members as they were completed. They were then considered line by line at meetings of the Commission. Often they were amended for good reason; sometimes they were amended because one Commissioner preferred another form of words for saying the same thing, and no one thought it mattered much either way. Sometimes a proposed change brought forth a defensive reaction from the drafter who thought that the change would be inaccurate or misleading. If he convinced the Commission, the draft survived: if he did not, new wording was adopted there and then, or if the passage was complicated, the drafter had to produce a new version in the next draft. And so it went on. For some chapters there were several revised drafts and several discussions. And there were appendices — more statistical tables, copies of questionnaires and covering letters.

For Fuller and myself and all our supporting staff, this was a far from easy time. As the nth draft was revised, amendments incorporated and sent for typing, its reappearance as draft $n + 1$ for checking before circulation would sometimes produce a weariness bordering on nausea. Junior staff after hours of checking masses of figures in seemingly endless tables found their eyes glazing over or failing to focus. But eventually one day in the late autumn the last page of the last chapter was cleared by the Commission and the report was sent to the Stationery Office for printing. It emerged in February 1960 as a fairly substantial blue covered volume of 346 pages addressed on the first page in appropriate formal language to Her Majesty the Queen. The report itself covered 158 pages and included 57 tables. The rest of the volume consisted of 155 pages of appendices, 26 pages of Professor Jewkes' memorandum of dissent and an index.

The Chairman organised a farewell dinner for members and staff of the Commission in Brown's Hotel. It was a happy occasion tinged with a trace of sadness. A big job had been successfully completed; but it would be our last meeting as a group. The Chairman, as always, was in good form. When coffee had been served he thought it was time for parlour tricks. He summoned a waiter and asked for an egg, 'How would you like it done, sir; boiled, fried, scrambled or poached?' 'None of them; just bring me an egg in its shell.' When the egg was borne in, he placed it in a wine glass and set another glass next to it so that they were touching. Then he asked us whether anyone could move the egg from one glass to another without touching it, without lifting the glass from the table — and without breaking the egg. There were many bright ideas, all unrealistic, and many jests, but no successful demonstration. Then Sir Harry, holding the base of each glass to keep it steady, blew down into the glass with the egg. The egg rose slightly on the cushion of air which he had created and then fell back. Amid shouts of encouragement, he puffed out his cheeks and blew again harder. The egg rose higher; but again gravity proved stronger than Sir Harry's puff and it fell back. He made us all try in turn; no one succeeded in lifting the egg up to the rim of the first glass and tipping it over into the second. His high spirits only slightly deflated, Sir Harry decided that the glass was not quite the right shape. Certainly it could be done: 'I have done it,' he assured us; and such was the power of his personality, we believed him. During the last three years he had not only inspired, exhorted and exhausted us; he had entertained us. And he entertained us to the last.

Chapter 6

Assistant Secretary in the Department

As the last pages of the Royal Commission report were being cleared for the printers, word came that as soon as I was released from the Commission I would be promoted to a vacant assistant secretary post in the Department — head of the hospital division in which I had served as a principal before going to the Commission. I would be responsible for work concerned not only with hospital doctors and dentists, but also with nurses, other professional staff and a variety of other functions. Such is the heady effect of news of promotion, I did not question myself, far less the departmental hierarchy, on whether it was desirable that I should continue in a field over which I had tramped for many years. True, I would not be limited to doctors and dentists. But might it not have been better to leave hospitals behind and move to some other field which I could survey with a fresh eye? With the greater part of my career still before me might there not have been advantage in widening my experience and avoiding any possibility of being regarded as too much of a specialist? Other things being equal, wide general experience is preferred to specialist experience at the higher levels of the administrative hierarchy. The filling of vacancies was often done not simply by promoting someone straight into the vacancy, but by arranging two moves, in which someone else is moved sideways in the same grade and the person promoted fills the consequential vacancy. Something on these lines could have been done on this occasion.

Rightly or wrongly, no such thoughts troubled me. I liked dealing with doctors and dentists; promotion was presumably an indication that my performance in that field was reasonably well regarded; and I had a liking, which only later I recognised to be a far too unadventurous liking, for known, familiar territory. I knew the staff who would be working for me as heads of the three branches for which I would be responsible; and I knew they would do a good job.

One day at the beginning of 1960 I settled myself in a room in St. Andrew's House. I looked around the fairly spacious apartment in which I would spend more of my waking hours than in my own home. The full range of furniture appropriate to an assistant secretary sat ready for use — an impressively large desk, a table round which small groups could gather for discussion, a stand for coats and hats (not mine, as I did not possess one), a bookcase, sundry chairs and a carpet. In those days — standards have risen since then — only assistant secretaries and upwards were honoured with carpets. There was a marvellous view across to Arthur's Seat, that mini-mountain sitting green and serene not far from the centre of the city. Several weeks were to pass before I realised how much cold wind slipped in through the bent steel frames of the ageing, east-facing windows.

As an assistant secretary I was provided with one additional facility more important by far than the better class of furniture — a personal secretary for my own exclusive use. In those days even principals had to rely on the typing pool, and their telephones were connected only to the general switchboard. Now Miss Wright (we were sparing in the early sixties in the use of Christian names) would be available to take dictation and reproduce my thoughts and revised versions of my thoughts in type at times convenient to me rather than at times determined by pressures on the typing pool. She had on her desk in a nearby room occupied by several personal secretaries a so-called Plan 7 telephone which enabled her to filter my incoming telephone calls and — even more useful — to connect me to colleagues and outside numbers without my looking up directories, trying again when my quarry was out of his office and trying yet again when the number was engaged.

When the Royal Commission report was published a week or two later neither the Government nor the professions could claim a famous victory. But criticisms were muted, and it was agreed by both sides that its proposals should be accepted as the basis for a new pay settlement. My colleagues and I, from the Ministry of Health and the Department, were immediately deep in discussion with the professional bodies about the detailed implementation of the Report. No one was disposed to niggle or cavil, and soon the Commission's proposals were translated into official notices instructing the health service boards and councils to pay at the new rates. The Government also announced its agreement to the appointment of a Review Body, as the Commission had recommended, to keep pay under review in future. History thus offered at least one example of the recommendations of a Royal Commission being implemented immediately.

Though questions of pay disappeared from the current agenda concerning doctors and dentists in hospitals, other problems remained. Some rather technical matters of grading had to be dealt with; there was growing interest in the arrangements for training consultants; and the number of consultants had to be increased if the specialist services were to expand in response to changes and developments in medicine and increasing public expectations. The general financing of the NHS was not then as much an issue of public controversy as it became many years later, and the increased funds available each year made possible a steady increase in the consultant establishment.

As the months went by, much of my time was spent on the nursing front. Here all was far from quiet. The old regime under which hospital nursing staff consisted largely of trained professional nurses and nurses in training had become increasingly outmoded. There was a growing need for 'pairs of hands' — auxiliary staff who were neither professional nurses nor in training to become professional nurses, but who were able to assist in practical everyday tasks after some basic training in the job. There were different views in the profession about how much training was needed, and about the desirable proportion of auxiliary to trained nurses. There were also different attitudes to the employment of part-time nurses, trained or untrained. The older generation of hospital matrons were inclined to resist this type of employment. No one, however, had any doubt that more trained nurses were required — on the one hand to deal with the additional nursing work resulting from doctors' capacity to treat conditions hitherto not treated; and on the other to compensate for increased holidays and reduction in the working week. And all the time, as there always had been, there was a steady loss of trained nurses through marriage and childbirth.

The Chief Nursing Officer, Miss Robinson, an ex-matron, as much respected in the Department as among her professional colleagues in the field, the principal concerned and I spent many hours round my table. We met representatives of the nursing profession and of the hospital boards, and we kept in touch with our colleagues in the south. We organised recruitment campaigns. The young ladies featured in the advertisements had to be reasonably attractive, but not so attractive as to stimulate criticism about unrealistic and glamorous advertising. It was sometimes difficult to get the balance right, but it could liven up a dull afternoon. We did not always make the kind of progress we would have wished, but some at least of the formidable ladies who made up the senior ranks of the profession were flexible and resourceful, and thanks to them some progress was made. In any event there was a steady increase in the numbers of nurses trained and untrained — though it did not seem to reduce the number of complaints from Parliament, the press and the public about the shortage of nurses.

Happily, in the early sixties there were no major conflicts about pay between the Government and the nursing profession of the kind which became all too frequent in later decades after inflation had taken off. Even then, however, I was aware that anyone, from Minister of the Crown to the humblest hospital functionary, involved in the administration of nursing services has to reckon with one particular problem not found in many other fields. In any disagreement or conflict with the nurses he is always at a disadvantage. Politicians, press and public are very ready to regard nurses as ministering angels, overworked and underpaid. Sometimes, some of them are overworked and underpaid; but not always, and probably no more than many people in other occupations. A few nurses may be ministering angels, and most of them do a good professional job; but there is no reason to think that nurses generally are more dedicated to their work than people in other professions. It is perhaps understandable that those who care for our relatives and friends — and no doubt for us too in the course of time — when they are ill, distressed or helpless, when money and possessions offer no comfort, should attract a special kind of sympathy. But it adds to the problems of administrators trying to be fair as between one group of people and another.

There was no comparable well of public support for another group with which I was concerned — the 'Professions Supplementary to Medicine'. These were the physiotherapists, radiographers, chiropodists and others who in different ways took part under doctors' supervision in the diagnosis or treatment of patients. (Prayers are often heard in church for doctors and nurses. How often are there prayers for radiographers — or for that matter hospital cleaners and all the other staff without whom hospitals would not function?) In 1960, there was passed the Professions Supplementary to Medicine Act which provided for the first time for the registration and the definition of the qualifications of members of these professions. While most of the work connected with the passing of this legislation was completed before I came on the scene, we began after its passing various efforts in association with the professional bodies to stimulate recruitment and extend training arrangements.

Hospitals are essentially buildings in which people needing certain kinds of care are brought in contact with the people able to provide it. While about two-thirds of hospital expenditure goes to pay those who provide that care and other supporting staff, a great deal of money has to be spent on constructing, equipping and maintaining the buildings. Much of the Department's responsibility for hospital buildings fell on my division. As a principal I had been involved in hospital building in one regional hospital board area, and I had not found it the most congenial part of my work. With more extensive responsibilities now, I found it no more congenial.

Many of my administrative colleagues found it interesting, and some found it exciting, to work with doctors, nurses, architects, engineers and surveyors in planning fine modern buildings — buildings which because of the work done inside usually involved intriguing complications unknown in simple structures like offices or schools. Why did I not share their enthusiasm? I was, as an administrator, more interested in people, policies and services than in bricks, mortar and associated objects. Planning new hospital units seemed to involve endless discussion not only to resolve ordinary differences of view, but also to prevent utopian visions and personal ambitions parting company with reality. Some weight had to be given to the views of consultants as potential users of premises, but sometimes a change of consultant could produce a marked change of attitudes and a return to the drawing board. I began to harbour a suspicion of architects and the fondness of some of them for the new, the untried and the eye-catching. (Architects have of course a special problem. In all professions there must be willingness to experiment with new ideas and methods; but architects' experiments cannot be poured down the sink or simply abandoned when shown to be unsuccessful. They stand for decades for all to mourn.) I had no doubts about the importance of the work; but I found myself more at home in other fields.

Other subjects, some mundane, some esoteric, came my way — cleaning services, catering services, blood transfusion, funds for medical research, radiological protection, hospital morbidity statistics. Who would have thought that morbidity statistics could be interesting and important? Hospitals at that time could provide figures showing how many patients they treated, but not what they were treated for, how long they had spent on a waiting list or how long they stayed in hospital. I found myself chairman of a group planning the introduction of a new computer based system of medical records which would give statistical information for Scotland as a whole and for individual hospitals about in-patients treated. We were not interested in collecting figures for the sake of collecting figures. We wanted information to be available about time on waiting lists and length of stay in order that these could be studied by people on

71

the ground. If waiting time was radically longer at hospital A than at hospital B for treatment of the same condition, why was this so? Could waiting times at A be reduced? (Waiting times are more important than numbers on waiting lists. If I am waiting for admission to hospital what matters to me is how long I have to wait, not how many other people are waiting as well.) If consultant X kept patients in hospital longer than other consultants working in the same field, this would be worth investigation — by consultant X and his colleagues, not any committee or administrative authority. Better statistical information of the kind we had in mind would, we thought, help those responsible for using hospital resources to examine whether they were using them most effectively. The BMA agreed, and cooperated in the exercise.

I had little personal contact with ministers during this period. There was, however, the usual steady diet of PQs and ministerial correspondence. Suggested replies to PQs were normally prepared by the principals or members of their staff; but the same departmental procedures were followed as in my early days as an assistant principal. Drafts were considered and sometimes amended not only by me as assistant secretary, but also by the under secretary under whom I worked and then the Secretary of the Department. A very few PQs raised difficult points but the vast majority did not. I suppose this virtual involvement of the whole departmental hierarchy was an acknowledgement of the traditional concept of Question Time as the great inquisition on the activities of the government and the bureaucracy. But the realities of the situation — the routine nature of most of the PQs; the very limited opportunity open to the MPs to pursue the matter and press the minister when other Questions are waiting to be answered; and the fact that drafts of other ministerial statements and speeches did not receive this level of treatment in the Department — made me sceptical about this use of official time.

The general run of ministerial correspondence did not involve anyone above assistant secretary before suggested replies appeared on ministers' desks, even although many letters from MPs to ministers raised more difficulties than PQs. An assistant secretary's in-tray was seldom without patches of greenery — the green folders containing the letters to ministers and draft replies prepared by principals or one of their juniors. As my division dealt with complaints about the treatment, in the general as well as the clinical sense, of patients in hospitals, many green folders coming to me contained letters from MPs or letters forwarded by them from their constituents complaining about long waits for admission, delays in out-patient departments, poor food, inadequate treatment by doctors or nurses, or premature discharge. My colleagues had obtained reports from the hospital boards — and sought further reports if the first seemed inadequate. On the basis of these reports and discussions with medical or nursing colleagues they had framed draft replies for the minister, rebutting, explaining or apologising as the facts seemed to warrant. Things can go wrong in hospitals as in other establishments; but granted the nature of the work done in hospitals the consequences can sometimes be distressing or even tragic. The minister had to be given an honest reply, as sympathetic as possible, and we had to bear in mind that in some of these cases litigation might follow.

Such changes as I made on the draft usually concerned the substance or the presentation rather than the style. I would never make a significant change in a draft dealing with the treatment of a patient without clearing it with any professional staff who had been involved. The folders were then sent on their way to the minister's private office. Sometimes his private secretary would ring to suggest a change or a different approach, but not often. Sometimes ministerial correspondence on a particular topic could develop into a long running saga with successive green folders being tied together and the whole tale becoming more complicated as allegations were made of inadequate investigation or cover-up (although I do not recall that particular phrase, now much beloved by press and anti-Government politicians, being used at that time). It was all in a day's work.

Sometimes an MP dissatisfied with the answer to a PQ or the contents of a minister's letter would 'seek to raise the question on the adjournment'. For half an hour each day after the end of the ordinary business of the House one Member had the opportunity, after giving notice, of raising a matter of concern to him or one of his constituents; and the appropriate minister had to be there to reply. I was involved in one or two such adjournment debates — preparing a draft speech for the minister, briefing him orally and being present during the debate in the official box. These adjournment debates are among the low points of Parliamentary life. They take place normally at 10 p.m. after a long day; and it is seldom that there are more than three members in the chamber — the Member raising the issue, the minister and a Parliamentary Private Secretary whose role it is to support the minister generally and in particular to convey any notes between the minister and the officials in the box. The general thrust of what the MP is going to say is almost always known in advance, and the minister has in his hand before the member even starts speaking the script of a speech which he can amend or reinforce in the light of what is said. It is all very predictable and because it is also very forgettable only one such occasion remains in my mind.

Not that I remember anything of the debate itself. What impressed it on my memory was not any challenge to government policy or the plight of some unfortunate constituent but what some might regard as a low concern about my personal convenience and comfort. My principal and I had prudently booked berths on the last sleeper train to Edinburgh leaving King's Cross about 1.00 a.m. There would be plenty of time to spare, we thought, after the end of the debate. During the afternoon we heard that a change in the evening's business in the House meant that the adjournment would not be moved until well after 10.00 p.m. How much later? No one knew. We paraded with the minister behind the Speaker's Chair at 10.00 p.m. and hoped for the best. The other business dragged on . . . and on. Provided, however, it finished by midnight we could still catch the train — just. By 11.45 we had given up hope. But just after midnight the earlier business suddenly collapsed. We nipped smartly into the box. Exactly half an hour later the debate came to an end. We sped downstairs, out into the courtyard and caught a taxi. We exhorted the driver to do his best, and he did. At King's Cross we rushed to the platform indicator and then the platform — only to see the red light on the back of the last carriage of our train getting smaller as it moved steadily away from us. After a few choice comments, we could only return to Dover House where there were beds in an attic for use in an emergency, doze for a few hours and then set off once more for King's Cross to catch the first morning train to Edinburgh. A splendid breakfast of the kind for which British Rail are justly renowned did something to restore morale.

If I had no reason to remember much about my few meetings with Scottish ministers, my only encounter about this time with an English minister remains clearly in my mind. It had fallen to me to look after the Scottish interest in a Bill before Parliament — the Human Tissue Bill, a Great Britain Bill dealing with the use of human tissue and organs for the care of patients and research. One day I learned that there was to be a meeting at the Ministry of Health to prepare for the second reading of the Bill. The minister himself, Mr Enoch Powell, would be in the chair and he had asked that Scotland should be represented. When I presented myself at his outer office I found that he had assembled, as was apparently his habit, an impressive array of top brass, Parliamentary, administrative, medical and legal. On the word being given, there filed into the minister's room the Parliamentary Secretary to the Ministry, the Government's Health spokesman in the House of Lords, the Parliamentary draftsman, the Chief Medical Officer, the Ministry's solicitor, the minister's private secretary, sundry other senior staff from the Ministry and me.

The minister went systematically down the text of that short Bill line by line, probing, commenting, questioning — questions about the use of human tissue, the problems of drafting, the attitude of members of the Upper House. I did not suppose there would be any questions for me in this high powered gathering. But the thorough, painstaking and penetrating Mr Powell did not forget that this was a Great Britain Bill. He fixed me with his eye and asked whether there were any particular Scottish implications or difficulties. Were any of the Scottish members of either House likely to raise any particular points? I was able to answer his questions apparently to his satisfaction. To my surprise he later expressed his thanks not in the off hand way adopted by some ministers in their dealings with officials (if, indeed, they offer any thanks at all) but with the same care and precision as had characterised his question. To the punctilious Mr Powell I was, I suppose, not just another official but the representative of the Secretary of State for Scotland, an equal partner with himself in the present exercise. In a few weeks, the Human Tissue Act 1961 was on the statute book.

Such contribution as I was able to make to a discussion about the issue of human tissue derived from close collaboration with doctors on the staff of the Department. It went without saying that the doctors had to be consulted and a common departmental view reached on any questions concerning the treatment of patients, the organisation of specialist services, the pay and conditions of service of doctors and the management of hospitals — and indeed on any subject involving doctors or the practice of medicine. On comparable questions involving dentists or nurses the Department's dental and nursing staff were involved. As so large a part of my work concerned the work of professional people in hospitals, seldom a day passed without a discussion or an exchange of minutes with one or more of my professional colleagues. In these exchanges we reached, sometimes easily, occasionally with difficulty, a common view on the line to be taken. While it was only administrators who put forward papers to ministers, it would have been a very brash administrator who proceeded without professional agreement in dealing with ministers, hospital boards, or anyone else on matters involving the professions. To safeguard against the possibility that some important aspect of the nation's health might be endangered by an unusually bold head of the Department recommending to ministers a course of action to which his medical colleagues were firmly opposed, there was an understanding that the Chief Medical Officer had, if he thought it necessary, direct access to the Secretary of State. I have never known a CMO take such action.

I enjoyed working with my professional colleagues. While they no less than the administrators were officers of the Secretary of State, the division of labour between us meant that while we had to be concerned primarily with the process and mechanics of government they were more concerned with the ends to which it was directed. This meant that although they were not, I think, any more humane or caring than we were, their responsibility was to think more about queues in the out-patient departments, the implications of new drugs, children with toothache and the care of bedfast old ladies than next week's debate in Parliament. And this could bring if not all human life, at least many interesting and sometimes poignant aspects of it into our mundane everyday exchanges. I found myself, too, sympathetic to what seemed to me to be the general ethos and outlook of the medical profession. Doctors in general do not see it as their role to create a brave new world; their aims are limited and practical. In spite of the vast extension of knowledge about the human mind and body and how they work, medicine is not an exact science; clinicians work with probabilities, possibilities and uncertainties. And no matter how well they look after their patients death comes as the end. A fifteenth century Frenchman described the role of the profession thus: 'To cure sometimes, to relieve often, to comfort always.' After five centuries and many changes, and even if it is not always honoured by every practitioner, that still seems a noble and a realistic aim today.

All this interest in doctors' work involved regular contact with the BMA. The very good relationship which the Department had with the BMA in Scotland derived from three principal factors. First, we hardly ever had to discuss anything so sordid as money; negotiations about pay and conditions were conducted on a Great Britain basis on the Whitley Council, with officials of the Ministry of Health taking the lead for the management side. Second, Scotland is not a large country, and contacts between St. Andrew's House and all kinds of professional and representative bodies tend to be less at arm's length than in the large scale, more impersonal, circumstances in which such relationships are conducted in the south. This does not inevitably produce sweetness and concord, but, other things being equal, tends to promote them. Third, Dr E.R.C. Walker, Scottish Secretary of the BMA, was personally more urbane and agreeable than some secretaries of representative bodies.

Edward Walker was a professional of the old school — charming in manner, devoted to high professional standards, and not entirely at home in the world of large organisations such as the NHS where so many aspects of professional employment were determined by a central authority. But any regrets he had about the establishment of a National Health Service were submerged by his concern to see reason and good sense prevail in its operation. I had first encountered him when I was an assistant principal in 1950, and by the time I was an assistant secretary had developed a close and personal relationship. We often met to discuss matters of common concern over coffee in his office or in mine. It might be the agenda for the next meeting between the Department and the Joint Consultants' Committee, an awkward dispute between a consultant and a hospital board, or a report prepared by a committee set up by the Scottish Health Services Council, a rather grand advisory body of which he and I were joint secretaries. If our discussions were relaxed and friendly, it did not mean that he was any less concerned to safeguard or to press the interest of his members — or that I was any less anxious to promote the interest of the Secretary of State and the public.

Neither Edward Walker nor my medical colleagues in the Department actually treated patients, but towards the end of 1961, I was brought into a close relationship with some senior consultants who did. At that time there were no generally accepted standards of staffing for the various specialities, and there were variations, sometimes marked variations, in the current standards in the different regions. While there could be no rigid conformity, the Department and representatives of the profession agreed that the time had come to devise some generally agreed staffing standards and reduce existing differences to what inevitably derived from geographical circumstances or the incidence of very specialised work. The Secretary of State appointed a committee to define these standards and to make recommendations for each of the five hospital regions about the number, type and distribution of posts required. Dr Joseph Wright, President of the Glasgow Faculty of Physicians and Surgeons, himself a physician with a special interest in cardiology, was appointed chairman; the other members were a professor of surgery, an obstetrician and gynaecologist, the physician superintendent of a mental hospital, the Senior Administrative Medical Officer of a regional hospital board and myself.

Throughout 1962 I spent a great deal of time as a member of the committee, which became known as the Wright Committee, going round the hospital regions and meeting representatives of medical staff, hospital boards and universities. We had to consider and then agree on what would be reasonable standards for each of the main specialities separately in relation to work load. For some specialities such as general medicine and general surgery this presented no major problem; for others, such as anaesthetics, radiology and laboratory medicine it was more difficult. There had to be special provision for teaching hospitals and for professorial units in these hospitals; and we had to take account of the particular problems of the more remote areas. By the beginning of 1963 we had not only devised staffing standards but had decided in the light of these standards what was the desirable number of consultants and support staff in each speciality in each region.

This bald account of the commmittee's work may suggest it was rather a dreary task for a layman not involved in the day to day work of hospital medicine. On the contrary I found it fascinating. Standards of staffing in, say, orthopaedic surgery or psychiatry could be determined only after hearing from orthopaedic surgeons and psychiatrists what they actually did — and then bringing a critical, sometimes sceptical, eye to bear in a field in which few laymen are called upon to venture. Our safaris throughout Scotland took us into not only the inevitable hospitals, offices and hotels but also many hospitable private homes, and we encountered a rich variety of human character. There were interesting insights into the human aspects of medicine: 'One of my most difficult jobs is to prevent my eager young men subjecting elderly patients to needless tests when they are going to die in a few days anyway.' Apart from that, the committee became, as all the best committees do, a club offering camaraderie and conviviality. There were characters and raconteurs among us, and laughter and good fellowship accompanied us on our travels.

Meanwhile, back in St. Andrew's House changes were taking place. In 1962 there was a reorganisation of departments within the Scottish Office. Secretaries of State for Scotland of whatever party had always regarded themselves in some sense as Scotland's ministers. Apart from the particular responsibilities laid on them by statute — for health, agriculture, housing, education and so on — they saw themselves as having a further if undefined responsibility for the general well being, especially the economic well being, of Scotland. Although most questions concerning industry and employment in Scotland were the responsibility of Whitehall ministers, the President of the Board of Trade and the Minister of Labour, the general public in Scotland expected the Secretary of State to be Scotland's general advocate and protector in such matters, and to be Scotland's voice when they were discussed in the Cabinet. The Scottish Home Department, in addition to dealing with the Secretary of State's statutory responsibilities for Police and Fire Services, had provided him with support for his activities in the general economic field. Increasingly it had been thought that the Scottish Office as a whole needed to do more to promote general economic prosperity; and the 1962 reorganisation was designed to make this possible by the creation of a new Scottish

Development Department. This department took over not only the economic functions of the Scottish Home Department but also the functions of other departments concerned with the economic infrastructure — housing, town and country planning, water and roads, most of this coming from the Department of Health for Scotland. As a consequence there was also created a Scottish Home and Health Department out of the remaining parts of SHD and DHS and these departments ceased to exist. As in many reorganisations, the same people continued to sit at the same desks. It was to the SHHD that I and my health service colleagues now belonged, though the day to day work on the administration of the NHS was unaffected.

Other changes had affected me intimately. I had started out in my assistant secretary role in 1960 with three entirely competent heads of branches — two principals and a senior executive officer — with whom I had a good working relationship. But staffing changes are always taking place in the Civil Service as a result of promotion, retirement and sideways moves to widen people's experience. By 1962 I had three different heads of branches. All were intelligent and in their different ways devoted to the public weal; but all in their different ways posed problems. This would have been bad enough in ordinary' circumstances. At a time when I had to be out of the office so much with the Wright committee and when as a result I had to delegate more than usual to heads of branches, the smooth and speedy despatch of official business suffered — and so did I. Let me give but one example. One of these individuals was what was called a 'direct entry principal', that is, he had come into the Civil Service at principal level after experience in other employment, in his case as a university lecturer. He was highly intelligent and hard working, but he found it difficult to accept that, in the short term at least, we had to work within the framework of general policy in which we found ourselves. If he was asked to produce a brief for a meeting next Thursday to deal with a particular problem, he might well say that we should not be having a meeting because the whole policy in the light of which this problem was to be considered was defective. In other words we should not be starting from here. Even if there were something to be said for his view of basic policy, we could not change it by next Thursday, and a brief was wanted — quickly. Argument ensued, patience wore thin and working relationships, not only with me, deteriorated. (Later when working for another assistant secretary the individual concerned realised the Civil Service was not for him. He returned to university life and did very well.)

All this did nothing to discourage the thought, now establishing itself in my mind for other reasons, that there might be something to be said for seeking pastures new. As my tally of years spent dealing with the NHS reached a bakers' dozen, I was beginning to feel that, agreeable as it was, my tendency of earlier years to cling to the known and the familiar (at least in my personal environment: intellectual horizons were not similarly constrained) seemed to be disappearing. While I had no clear idea where I wanted to go, it certainly seemed that it was about time for a change.

When the annual circular about sabbatical leave opportunities for civil servants came on my desk I did not as in previous years give it a quick glance and drop it in the waste paper basket. Was it perhaps worth considering in particular the possibility of a Nuffield Travelling Fellowship? This allowed whoever was appointed as Fellow to spend up to a year studying a subject of relevance to the work of his department. One Commonwealth country had to be included. The Fellowship made apparently generous financial provision not only for the Fellow but also for his or her spouse to travel as well. The Wright committee was very near completion of its work and there seemed to be no reason, official or domestic, why I should not spend a year away from St. Andrew's House with the prospect of employment in some other field on my return.

But what would be my field of study? Having asked myself that question and rejected several possible answers, I found a better one beginning to take shape. What about 'The Professions and the State'? As the boundaries of state activity extended and brought it into ever increasing contact with people who were members of independent self-governing professions, all sorts of important and interesting questions arose. To what extent, if at all, should governments control entry to and training for the professions? What problems result when professional people responsible for their own professional decisions are employed in services provided by the state for the public? As I knew only too well from experience of dealing with several professions, the possibilities for conflict are never far away. Why not study the experiences of some other countries? Such a study would certainly be relevant to the work of the Scottish Home and Health Department in organising the NHS in Scotland, spending millions of pounds of public money in so doing and becoming almost a monopoly employer of people in certain professions.

I consulted senior colleagues, gained their support and sent off an application form. The committee responsible to the Treasury for selecting the holder of the fellowship consisted of Sir Keith Murray, chairman of the University Grants Committee, and several heads of government departments. I was summoned for interview at the office of the UGC in Belgrave Square. I had never attended a selection board since my appearance before the Final Selection Board of the Civil Service Commission in 1947. As on that occasion I was led up a grand staircase to the interview room by a messenger. On this occasion the electricity and the heating were in full working order, and the messenger was a fairly sprightly mover. Although a fairly sprightly mover myself, I had learned by experience never to rush upstairs before entering a meeting. I had arrived needlessly breathless in an august gathering many years before after bounding up several flights of stairs. Thereafter I followed the advice of a medical colleague who was wont to say, 'Never run upstairs except for fire or haemorrhage.' I entered the room in good order and settled down to what turned out to be an agreeable exchange.

The main questioning was undertaken by Dame Evelyn Sharp, Permanent Secretary of the Ministry of Housing and Local Government, who later had a starring role in 'The Crossman Diaries'. I explained what I had in mind. Why did I chose Canada, Norway, Sweden, Denmark and France as the countries to be visited? I had to visit one Commonwealth country, and in the different Provinces of Canada different systems of health care showed different relationships between governments and the health professions. Indeed, in one Province, Saskatchewan, there had recently been — unheard-of thing — a doctors' strike. Norway, Sweden and Denmark were all interested in the provision of extensive social welfare services and all employed doctors and other professional people in these services on an apparently harmonious basis. Was it really as harmonious as it seemed? In France, which had until recently combined weak short-lived governments with a strong administrative structure, the tradition of individual liberty was particularly strong; and no doubt a study of relations between the professions and the state would yield some interesting material. Committee members did some more probing and questioning, but I got the impression that they were well disposed to my proposal.

A few days later after my return to Edinburgh I was pleased to learn that I had been awarded a Fellowship.

Chapter 7

Sabbatical Leave Abroad

On the evening of 1st May 1963 my wife and I boarded the *Queen Elizabeth* in Southampton Docks. The age of the great liners providing regular services across the Atlantic was not yet near its end, and we looked forward to six days of comfort and relaxation at sea. As we stretched out on our deck chairs next morning, watching the coast of England slip slowly away, I thought of the labours of the last few weeks and what lay ahead in North America.

On a visit to the Treasury soon after the announcement of the award of the Nuffield Travelling Fellowship I had discussed the rules and practical arrangements for my period of sabbatical leave. There was not much to be learned. The only requirement was that I should write a report on my chosen theme. How I organised my studies; how much of the year I spent abroad; where I went in the chosen countries; how I identified and got access to the people most likely to enlighten me; how I spent the money available (though not a penny more) — all that was left to me.

I had taken up offers of help from Dr Kenneth Cowan, Chief Medical Officer of the Department, and Dr Edward Walker of the BMA. The former had written to his opposite numbers in Canada and the other countries I was to visit, and as a result I had been put in touch with people in the various Health Ministries who would arrange programmes of interviews and visits. Edward Walker, too, had written to his contacts in these countries, and I was assured of hearing not only official views and those of professional bodies but also those of some practitioners in the field. It was clear that my interest would be concentrated on the health professions. It was in the health field more than any other that governments had significant relations with professional bodies because of their desire to make, or to see that someone made, the services of professional people available to the population at large. They had no such concerns in relation to, say, accountants or architects. In a limited way governments were involved with the legal profession in the provision of legal aid, and I had also managed to arrange one or two contacts in that field. While my wife and I are both members of that apparently small minority of Scots people who have no relatives in Canada, I had written to some friends now resident there; and friends in Edinburgh had invited us to get in touch with their Canadian friends and relations. We would as a result have at least some social contacts as well as rounds of visits to offices (for me) and to art galleries and shops (for my wife).

After talking to many people, consulting books, brochures and time-tables, writing to British Embassies in Denmark, Norway, Sweden and France, visiting the Canadian High Commission and the offices of the Canadian Pacific Railway in London, I had made a plan for the next few months. We would spend ten weeks in Canada visiting Ottawa, the Federal capital, and five of the ten Provinces (health is primarily a Provincial matter); three weeks at home reflecting, resting and preparing for the next stage; three weeks in Denmark and two each in Norway and Sweden; and finally after another short break at home, three weeks in France. I knew who would be my initial contacts in Ottawa and the Provincial capitals and how long we would spend in each of these places. I lay back in my deck chair and thought of these as yet unknown individuals ringing perhaps reluctant colleagues and persuading them to spend some time with an itinerant Scot when they had, I was sure, more pressing things to do.

Meanwhile, after several busy weeks — I had had my ordinary work to do as well as to make plans for travel to distant places — all the delights of the *Queen Elizabeth* were to be enjoyed. We had opted for Cabin Class, a half-way house between the splendours of First and the mundane utility of Tourist. Attentive stewards would wrap rugs round our legs when we lowered ourselves onto our appointed deck chairs. I discovered I had a great capacity for lying back and doing nothing except gaze at the far horizon. But there were bursts of activity — a game of traditional shuffleboard, conversation with fellow passengers, a swim in the pool, a walk round the deck. The sea air whetted appetites which were more than satisfied by what was offered in the dining saloon. In the evenings we danced to the music of the dance band days. . . . And the next day we did the same things all over again.

But one morning we docked in New York. After a few days with old university friends now dispensing learning at Princeton we continued our journey to Canada. I remember little of that day in the train from New York to Montreal through up-state New York except constant rain, a glimpse of a sign

'Ticonderoga' which was a sudden flash-back to almost forgotten history lessons at school, and the very heavy-handed customs and immigration formalities as the Canadian frontier approached. (It had been just as heavy-handed when landing at New York. North Americans can be as tiresomely and as rudely bureaucratic as anyone.) At Montreal another train, in which the prevailing language seemed to be a curious kind of French, took us to Ottawa.

Next day I had my first experience of what was to become my work routine for the next few months. At the hotel, I picked up a map of the town; identified the site of the office to which I was to report; presented myself at the appointed hour; had a general talk with my official host about my programme for the next few days; and then moved on to my first appointment. After a week of going the rounds of the offices of the Federal Government, talking to officials, some relaxed and forthcoming, others more formal and restrained, I knew something about the government of Canada, its health services and how professional people were employed. My wife and I also followed up some non-official contacts, were well entertained and learned about some aspects of Canadian life not described in official documents. Our hosts too learned something about Britain, including the apparently astonishing fact that not all Scots liked Scotch.

During the next couple of months we travelled right across Canada, over a short stretch of the Pacific to Victoria, capital of British Columbia on Vancouver Island, and then back to Montreal and Quebec. On the way west we visited Winnipeg, the capital of Manitoba, and Regina, the capital of Saskatchewan. Our fondness for what were becoming old-fashioned methods of transport led us to travel by train. We rolled westwards by stages on the gleaming air-conditioned coaches of *The Canadian*, the trans-continental train of the Canadian Pacific Railways. At each stop white-jacketed black attendants stood at the doors of the coaches while passengers took the chance of sniffing the air and stretching the legs. Some of these places had colourful evocative names — Medicine Hat, Swift Current, Moose Jaw. The reality on the other side of the tracks was, as far as we could judge, less picturesque. On we would go, enjoying the comfort of our 'bedroom' made down as a private sitting room during the day, or the 'dome car' of which the higher floor level and glass roof offered uninterrupted views all round.

Not that there were always exciting things to see. Far from it. Much of the time there was a terrible sameness about the scenery. For hour after hour of the journey to Winnipeg we had passed through the 'shield' country, a low, slightly undulating land of rock, scrub and trees with only an occasional forlorn

85

habitation to be seen. West of Winnipeg the prairies stretched flat and featureless to the horizon. I was encouraged to work my way through the piles of documents which helpful people had pressed upon me. Interest in the landscape quickened when the Rockies loomed into view. But all too soon darkness fell and the mountains disappeared into the night. We saw more of the magnificent Rockies on the return journey in the Canadian National Railway's less glamorous coaches on their parallel line further north. Could both these lines survive, I wondered, as passengers increasingly turned to aircraft or fast road transport? We were indeed near the end of an era, and now no passengers can sit or sleep their way right across Canada on either line.

As the weeks went by I became a connoisseur of offices, their reception arrangements, their inhabitants and in the ways they reacted to a visitor. Many government offices were in the Legislative Buildings — spacious stone structures, invariably surmounted by a soaring dome which had been built in Provincial capitals to house both the Provincial Legislature and Provincial Government offices. As the volume of government business and the number of bureaucrats increased, other more utilitarian glass and concrete structures were built to house those for whom there was no room under the same roof as the legislators. Professional associations too had their offices, some fairly opulent, some modest; and on the campuses of universities and hospitals I met professors, doctors, dentists and 'directors of nursing services' (matrons disappeared from hospitals in Canada before they retreated here). The insides of these varied buildings were seldom different from interiors at home; but the words 'Please remove your rubbers' which sometimes graced the front door reminded me that I was in a land where, only a few weeks before, the last of the winter-long snows had disappeared.

The people I met were almost invariably kind and helpful. They were generous with their time and their experience, and discussions often continued at their invitation in the canteens, restaurants or clubs. There were a few 'characters' among them but not many. There were certainly a few rugged and, I suspected, awkward individuals in Saskatchewan, and I speculated on the part played by personal factors in precipitating a doctors' strike during the previous year. Sometimes there would be a coolness or awkwardness as an interview began — visiting firemen, after all, do nothing to reduce the pile in the in-tray — but usually the atmosphere became more relaxed as I tried to establish some kind of rapport. None of these individuals had, I am sure, in their job descriptions responsibility for 'The Professions and the State'. But they all dealt in some way with services or activities involving public authorities and the professions, and I could pursue my theme only by listening to them describe these services and activities and by encouraging them to reflect upon the issues which arose. Some of them were eager to reflect more generally on the Canadian way of life or enquire about life in Britain, and I did nothing to discourage such turns in the conversation.

None of this could be described as hard work in the ordinary sense, but after about five weeks of moving from one place to another, meeting several new people each day, and talking to them about matters on which they were expert and I was ill-informed, I began to feel rather jaded. I had had my fill of mental health in Manitoba and workmen's compensation in Saskatchewan. In some of the hotels in which we had stayed we had encountered 'conventions', and some of the participants had not seemed to care about the sleep of non-participants. In spite of the hospitality of old friends now resident in Winnipeg, and a long weekend among the splendours of Banff National Park, I found myself in Vancouver feeling fed up and far from home. I realised more acutely than before the wisdom of those responsible for deciding the conditions of the Fellowship in making it possible for the wife to accompany the husband. Without my wife's companionship the prospect of the long haul back eastward would have been bleak indeed.

That evening we were royally entertained by my official host and his wife, and morale improved. The rehabilitation process was encouraged by a few days in Jasper National Park in the Rockies. I had my second wind. There were rounds of visits in Saskatoon and Toronto on the way east before arriving later in July in French Canada.

In Montreal and Quebec there were new factors present in all the talks and interviews — the language question and the politics of French Canada. This did not affect me personally; the mainly French speaking but bilingual people whom I met assumed our conversations would be in English — and were slightly surprised when occasionally I volunteered a few words in French. Although these questions of language and possible separation were in some ways disturbing — there were some violent incidents during our stay in Canada — they certainly provided a new intellectual stimulus to the visitor; and the physical character of Quebec City, more French than North American, was a welcome reminder of Europe. During these last few days of our tour the weather was for that part of Canada uncharacteristically hot (94°F each day) and very humid. We were not sorry to board the *Empress of Britain* in Montreal on 1st August and sail down the St. Lawrence bound for Greenock.

As on the outward voyage three months before, there was time for rest and reflection. I was taking back a host of impressions and recollections of Canada — its landscape, its public services. The most powerful and pleasant recollection was the kindness and hospitality of the people. Not only had I myself been looked after and entertained, the wives of my official hosts had invariably sought out my wife, shown her the sights and entertained her in their homes. In addition to all the material for the report which in due course I would write, I had a mass of information and reflections on the other subjects — the effect of the climate on human affairs (in the Provinces of central Canada it is very hot in summer and very cold in winter); the mechanics of Federal systems of government; the special problems of communities divided by language; the consequences of mixing fairly large immigrant populations (in Canada — Ukranian, Icelandic, Italian and others).

But in spite of the kindness and hospitality, I had never felt at home in Canada as I had earlier on holiday in various parts of Europe. I could certainly never have contemplated settling there as many people from Britain, and especially from Scotland, have done. Why not? The sameness of the landscape (while the shield was very different from the prairie there were hundreds of miles of each looking much the same); the modern city centres; the sense that life began if not yesterday certainly not much more than a hundred years ago. Except at the resorts of Banff Springs and Jasper, the local scene, urban or suburban, had never encouraged me to think of indulging in one of my favourite occupations — going out for a walk. All of which probably says more about me than it does about Canada.

During three weeks at home we dealt with a mass of mail, tried to restore order to the garden and made contact with friends and relatives. Then we boarded at Leith an Icelandic ship, the *Gullfoss*, which at that time provided regular services from Reykjavik to Copenhagen via Leith. Our car was lifted by crane from the dockside, enveloped in canvas and parked on the open deck. The *Gullfoss* was, not of course, a luxury liner, and the one facility which she offered and which the *Queen Elizabeth* did not — a Bible in Icelandic in the berth-side drawer — made no contribution to our life on board. After about 36 hours at sea we docked at Copenhagen on a damp, grey August morning as workers in overalls were making their way to docks and shipyards. Disembarkation was quick and uncomplicated, and by the time the first office workers were on the streets I was driving nervously for the first time along the right hand side of the road hoping to find the hotel in which we had booked for three nights.

SABBATICAL LEAVE ABROAD

We had thought that as we were to be about three weeks in Copenhagen it would be nice if we could find some furnished accommodation rather than stay the whole time in a hotel. Later that morning as I was paying my first visit to the offices of my hosts in the Danish Health Service Headquarters my wife was visiting offices of a different kind. In one of the estate agents' offices she learned that a small bungalow in the northern suburb of Virum was available for the period we required. Happily, no appointment had been fixed for me that afternoon. With the help of a large scale map we drove in pouring rain to Virum, found the house, decided it would suit us very well and reached an agreement with the owner, a pleasant elderly lady who was bound for Mediterranean sunshine. By mid-afternoon we felt we had already had a very successful day in what was no longer a strange city.

After that very wet start, we enjoyed three weeks of fine early autumn weather in what soon became one of our favourite cities. I would leave our suburban retreat each morning, sometimes by car, sometimes by train, for my daily round of visits. There seemed no unseemly pressure of traffic, and when I had the car, there seldom seemed to be difficulty in finding a parking space. But it was a pleasant place in which to walk about, to enjoy the mellow old buildings and suddenly catch sight of the sea at the end of a street. At weekends we drove into the country and saw trim fields, great castles, tiny harbours, and fairy tale villages.

We were sorry to leave. Fine modern car ferries departed daily for Oslo from the centre of Copenhagen, but we took the chance of seeing more of Denmark by going the long way round — by road and ferry via Odense (where Hans Christian Anderson came from), Veijle (where much of British bacon comes from) and the university town of Aalborg — to Frederikshavn in North Jutland. From there a far from modern steamer took us overnight to Oslo.

After a week of doing the rounds in Oslo, a more rugged place than Copenhagen, we drove to Stockholm, changing from the right to the left side of the road at the frontier between Norway and Sweden. (Not long after, the Swedes changed to right hand drive at vast expense.) In Stockholm we were based in sumptuous self-catering accommodation attached to an excellent modern hotel looking out over one of the arms of the sea which embrace the city. Stockholm was much more expensive than Oslo or Copenhagen, and the traffic and fly-overs reminiscent of North America. There was a cool modern urbanity about the place, tempered, however, by the presence of many fine old buildings and the awareness that this was the capital city of an ancient northern kingdom.

Two weeks later we drove back to Oslo through long empty miles of fields and woods. Then after one final week with the Norwegians we headed for home.

Eight weeks in Scandinavia had been interesting and revealing in many ways. In Britain, we were, and still are, accustomed to think of Norway, Sweden and Denmark as modern progressive countries providing advanced arrangements for social welfare and often leading contemporary fashion in architecture and internal design. True enough; but they are also old countries, monarchies indeed, in which tradition and history still play a major part. Although Norway became independent only in 1905, it had earlier been part of the Swedish, and before that the Danish, kingdom. Each has a long established official body responsible for the oversight and provision of health services — a kind of quango, separate from, if under the general control of, the government minister responsible for health. In Denmark, this body known as the National Health Service dates from 1803; in Sweden the National Medical Board is even older and celebrated its 300th anniversary in 1963. This long tradition of government activity in the health field is one reason why there did not seem to be the same suspicion of the exercise of state authority in this field as there had been in Great Britain until recently and still was in North America.

It was the health service organisations who were my hosts. They were used to visitors from many parts of the world and had well-oiled procedures for dealing with them. Everyone I met spoke English, some with astonishing fluency. I went the rounds of officials in these organisations, government departments and professional organisations — sometimes in stark modern offices, sometimes in comfortable old-fashioned rooms in ancient buildings with sofas against the wall and cigars on the table. Hospitals too were on my itinerary, and though the object was to meet individuals working there, I saw something of the hospitals themselves. One large, new and glossy establishment on the outskirts of Copenhagen was so accustomed to receiving official visitors that a lady was employed full-time to show them round. In the middle of all the bright modern efficiency I was surprised to see shades of the workhouse; all up-patients wore a standard hospital uniform — grey linen suits for the men and print frocks and white stockings for the women. At another modern hospital in Stockholm I saw an example of a not particularly modern form of personal transport as nurses propelled themselves along the corridors on scooters.

In Copenhagen I was able to make contact with the legal world and learn something about the legal profession and its relation with the public authorities in the provision of legal aid. I could not pursue this in any detail but it gave me at least a whiff of another aspect of professional life in Denmark. And though it did not extend my knowledge or experience in any significant way, I sat for a while one morning through largely incomprehensible exchanges in a civil court after the judge had — so I was told — greeted me from the bench and welcomed a visitor from across the sea.

On many occasions I had lunch as guest of my hosts. Sometimes open sandwiches would be delivered from the canteen, or even brought out from the depths of a briefcase. For all their reputation for a certain aloofness the Swedes were by no means the least hospitable. In Stockholm, I was taken to several restaurants, and it was only in Stockholm that my wife and I were invited to anyone's home. In Oslo there was one curious lapse from the usual pattern. I turned up for a meeting fixed for midday and departed about 1.30 after a friendly talk which was entirely satisfactory save in one respect — there was no mention, far less offer, of food or drink.

As in other parts of the world, bureaucrats in Scandinavia, whether in official or professional organisations, do not always conform to stereotype; and apart from encountering many varieties of personality and demeanour I met some colourful characters. The first in this category was probably not as colourful as I thought she was. Early in my stay in Copenhagen I visited a senior and very formidable looking lady in the nursing profession. As I listened to what she was telling me about the employment of nurses, I noticed in her bookcase several volumes entitled *Dansk Lov*. '*Dansk*', I knew meant 'Danish', and '*lov*' could presumably only mean 'love'. I looked again at the lady behind the desk and for a few moments was oblivious to what she was saying. I had heard of the liberated attitude of Scandinavians in sexual matters, but surely . . . I dragged my mind back to the recruitment of nurses. As soon as I was out of her door, I took out my Danish dictionary. How easy it is sometimes to jump to wrong conclusions. '*Lov*', I read, means 'law'. I was later to see many other bookcases full of '*Dansk Lov*'.

Once in Stockholm I lost my way when driving to a hospital on the outskirts of the city where I was to have lunch with a distinguished professor who was head of the medical school. Having found the hospital I had to find his office, and when at last I knocked on his door I was at least fifteen minutes late. A large figure opened the door and boomed: 'Ah Scotchman, I am waiting for you.' I was not sure whether this was a welcome or a reprimand. But after a few minutes eating and drinking at his table, there was little doubt that he was enjoying talking to me. As the lunch progressed our discussion became more and more relaxed and animated. When eventually we parted with expressions of mutual esteem, he gave me his home telephone number 'in case you have any more questions'.

On one of our last days in Oslo I had an early afternoon appointment with an official in one of the government departments. When our discussion came to an end he said that the permanent secretary of the department would like to see me. I was taken to his office. Not only did this lively engaging individual want to see me, he wanted to take me out to a restaurant — in mid-afternoon! I said I had arranged to meet my wife. No problem; she must come too. And so at 4.00 p.m. on an otherwise grey Nordic afternoon a party of four was to be found in a well known Oslo restaurant washing down splendid helpings of smoked salmon with liberal quantities of white wine. We talked about everything except the matters which had brought me to Oslo. The permanent secretary was very interested in life in Great Britain and, unlikely as it was, had some official reason for being particularly interested in football pools. I had to confess considerable ignorance of this important aspect of British life. But there were other aspects of the current scene in Britain and Norway which kept us all lively until we had eaten our fill of smoked salmon and drunk all the wine that was good for us. My wife and I dined very simply that evening.

A couple of days later we travelled back from Oslo to Newcastle on one of the elegant white mini-liners of the Olsen Line (which like the *Queens* of Cunard, the *Empresses* of the Canadian Pacific and the modest *Gullfoss* no longer provide regular leisurely and comfortable crossings of the oceans). In Edinburgh I sorted out notes and reflections while my wife had the more urgent task of sorting out the laundry. We paid the waiting bills, assured ourselves that all was well with elderly relatives, bought tickets for yet another journey, and early in November set off for Paris.

There we spent three weeks in a comfortable but not luxurious hotel in a central area off the Rue de Rivoli. My official host was the Ministry of Health whose main office occupied an elegant nineteenth century block at the top of the Champs Élysées looking across to the Arc de Triomphe over the swirling mass of traffic. Its wonderful site and impressive exterior belied a rather gloomy and awkward interior relieved by magnificent views from the principal rooms. I had my introductory talk with officials whose helpfulness was edged with the slightly distant formality which I came to recognise as typical of many French officials. A skeleton programme already prepared was filled out and I was launched on my study of parts of *la vie Parisienne* unknown to the tourist.

That study introduced me in the next three weeks to the occupants of many of the rooms in the Ministry building, as they expounded, explained and answered my questions. There seemed to be a higher proportion of women in fairly senior posts than would be found in a government department in Britain. (I later learned that some parts of the French higher civil service are much more equal than others, and there were unlikely to be so many women in prestigious groups such as the Inspectors of Finance and the Prefects and their assistants.) I found my way to other government offices and the offices of professional bodies and various parts of Paris. If the offices and officials of the French equivalent of the General Medical Council and the British Medical Association were testimony to the power and the prosperity of the medical profession in France, the cramped offices of the nursing organisation in a back street was some indication of the relatively low standing and influence of the nurses, at least at that time.

I moved about the city by metro or on foot. I was intrigued, not for the first time, by the evocation of past glories in the names of so many of the streets and metro stations. Statesmen, warriors and battles had their memorials on indicator boards, signs, plans and on the lips of millions of Parisians. I was intrigued too that in the land of *égalité* there were two classes of metro passenger — though the anarchic strain in the French character resulted in first class coaches being invaded from time to time by some whose demeanour did not suggest an eagerness to pay for privilege. There was usually something interesting to see when going about on foot. As I left the Ministry's offices on some of these early winter afternoons, the lights were on, and I would walk back to the hotel down the Champs Élysées or the Faubourg St. Honoré noting the affluence on display in the glittering shop windows.

As in other places, hospitals, or particularly some members of their staffs, figured in my itineraries. To the lay eye large general hospitals are distinguished from one another only by the age and style of the buildings. One central Paris hospital of great renown and distinction remains in my mind only because there seemed a certain scruffiness about the beds; it was not apparently the custom to iron the pillowslips. One ancient foundation on the outskirts of the city keeps its place in my memory because of a marvellous old pharmacy with porcelain jars and bottles of wonderful colour and design.

But Paris is not France, even although there is more central control from the capital than in most western countries. My hosts suggested I should see something of a Département at work and I gladly spent a day in Orléans. I was happy too to take a day off like everyone else on 11th November and see another aspect of French life as the Armistice Day parade came down the Champs Elysées and General de Gaulle stood in an open car waving to the populace.

As the days went by I found in my encounters with officials and professional people confirmation of what I remembered about certain strands in French history and politics. The revolutionary tradition glorifying liberty was alive and well. The 'liberal' professions were suspicious of state power and any restrictions on their freedom. At the same time, idealised concepts of *La France* and *La Gloire* gave the state, if not the government, a certain prestige and distinction. The Civil Service was a formally constituted part of the state machinery with its own separate identity and not merely the arm of the government as in Great Britain. Indeed, until the recent establishment of the Fifth Republic under General de Gaulle only the strong centralised bureaucracy had kept the country going while one weak government followed quickly on the fall of another. There had to be, it was generally acknowledged, some restrictions on liberty — but of what nature and how were they to be determined? Not very profound or unusual sentiments; but perhaps the basic problem is highlighted in France where it is the habit to analyse, expound and set it all out in writing.

That habit of careful analysis and exposition in writing is followed not only in relation to the classical problems of political philosophy but also in dealing with practical everyday problems. When I asked for a brief indication of how a particular situation was dealt with, I was very often referred to a *texte de base*. Such was the concern to have a text, that it sometimes seemed to me that unless there was a text describing it, no situation would be allowed to exist. Alternatively, the response to my question would begin '*En principe* . . '; and there would follow a careful explanation of the general rules. But then I was usually told: '*il y a des dérogations*', and there followed a list of exceptions which sometimes seemed to leave the basic principle in a very insecure and vulnerable state. These habits of thought and exposition, rather different from the more empirical approach of my compatriots, were perhaps to be expected in a country where philosophy is a school subject in which at least some pupils are examined for four hours at a stretch.

After some early apprehension I was encouraged to find that I could follow these expositions, or most of them, in French, and I could make in French what seemed from the replies to be appropriate responses and comments. I had, after all, done six years of French at school and one at university, and had been able to have reasonably relaxed chats with French friends. But during the first few days of my visit, before I had became acclimatised to the language of the official world, the concentration required for hours on end had produced a considerable strain, and I tottered back to the hotel feeling quite exhausted. I had not expected that anyone would be anxious to speak in English and with one exception my expectations were well founded. After all in Whitehall or St. Andrew's House it would certainly be assumed, except in the most unusual circumstances, that any visitor would understand English. While few of my hosts spoke in the slow measured cadences of General de Gaulle, who always made the French language if not French policies beautifully clear for Anglo-Saxons, most were considerate and understanding. As I was leaving after my last visit, the doorkeeper with whom I had often passed the time of day, told me he had thought I was French Canadian. In all the circumstances I took this as a compliment.

Our three weeks flew past. Enjoyable leisure hours were spent with hospitable French friends. From them we learned about aspects of French life which would not find a place in the report which very soon I would have to start to write. On Friday 22nd November we boarded the Night Ferry at the Gare du Nord and slept our way in a Wagon Lit across the Channel. (Another form of transport which exists no more.) When the dining car was attached to the train at Dover we went along for breakfast. The morning papers had come on board and banner headlines proclaimed 'Kennedy Assassinated'.

But life went on. Back at home in Edinburgh I settled down after a few days to write my report. I had brought back many documents of different kinds from different countries; I had notes of all my discussions and visits; and I had a host of recollections and impressions. All this had to be sorted out so that I could sketch the outlines of a report which would identify, describe and comment on the main issues. I worked away at home for the next few weeks drafting and re-drafting in long-hand. I made arrangements at the office for the typing and final production of what was going to be a fairly substantial report. I rather enjoyed not going out on winter mornings and settled down to this novel form of domestic activity.

Some time early in March I finished the last chapter and the report was produced in 'off-set litho' by HMSO. It was indeed a fairly substantial document — more than 50,000 words. There was no question of publication, but copies were sent not only to the Treasury, as was required, but also to various libraries, people who had particularly helped me and others in government departments, professional bodies and elsewhere whom I thought would be interested.

The report described the ways in which entry to and practice in the professions was controlled by governments or legislation in the countries I had visited. This is a fairly straightforward aspect of government/professional relationships in which all the battles now lay in the past. More of the text was devoted to the description and assessment of the ways in which governments and government appointed bodies arranged for the services of professional people to be available to the citizens — a much more difficult area in which controversy still simmers and occasionally erupts, especially over remuneration. I tried to deal with the main practical problems facing politicians, administrators and the professions themselves, how the inevitable disagreements are to be kept within reasonable grounds and how satisfactory relationships are to be achieved. There were of course no simple panaceas and I could offer no blinding new insights — only a series of points, none of them very surprising, which governments on the one hand and professions on the other ought to observe.

The value of sabbatical leave as distinct from other kinds of study or investigation is not, however, to be judged by the quality of the report produced or any tally of lessons learned or implemented. It exists to do something, albeit not easily defined, for the individual. I was certainly better informed at the end of my leave; but that was not presumably the object. The hope of those introducing schemes of sabbatical leave is no doubt that the individuals benefiting from them will have existing patterns of thought challenged, will look at problems against a broader frame of reference, will be generally intellectually stimulated, and will return after a period away from day-to-day responsibilities all the more capable of assuming more responsibility — not necessarily in the same field. The investment in sabbatical leave for one person can be considerable — not only the £2,000 expenses, as it was in my case, but also the regular succession of monthly salary cheques during the period of absence.

Was all this justified by changes in me or by improved performance when I returned to the treadmill? The individual concerned may be the least able to judge. Any intellectually sensitive individual changes and develops as the years go by. He may find it difficult to be sure about the origin or reason for some of the changes. Certainly I think my frame of reference was extended. And I hope Lord Nuffield would have thought his money had not been wasted.

Chapter 8

Byways and Back Rooms

All departments, according to Civil Service lore, have their salt mines — forgotten backwaters well away from the main stream of public and political interest where the daily grind is just as hard, sometimes harder, but less interesting and rewarding than elsewhere. An exaggeration perhaps, but in the spring of 1964 on my return to the office, it certainly seemed to me that I had been banished to Siberia.

In the last weeks of my period of sabbatical leave I had naturally wondered where I would be employed when I returned to ordinary departmental work. It was unlikely that I would be implementing any lessons derived from my study of the relations between the professions and the state. The Health Service side of the Scottish Home and Health Department was the only part of the Scottish Office concerned in any significant way with these issues; and I had no desire, nor was it practicable, merely to return, in the short term at least, from whence I came. Sabbatical leave was designed primarily to enlarge horizons and to stimulate generally, and I looked forward to pastures new and challenging somewhere else in the Scottish Office.

Since the reorganisation of departments in the Scottish Office in 1962, SHHD had had as Principal Establishment Officer an under secretary who combined general oversight of all personnel and allied matters with other duties. There was also an assistant secretary full time on establishment work. Both came from the old Scottish Home Department, and I did not know them very well. When I met them to discuss my future I did not expect them to welcome me with joyful enthusiasm, but I was not prepared for the dispiriting reception which I received. It seemed that I was something of a problem. There was, I was told, no obvious vacancy into which I could be fitted. But the

Department had to keep up the progress on civil defence planning. At present there was one civil defence division under an assistant secretary with several branches. What had been decided was that I should be a second civil defence assistant secretary and should take responsibility for some of these branches.

This was put to me by the under secretary in a rather perfunctory and weary sort of way. Although later I grew to respect him, he showed on that day little skill in man-management. My reaction was far from perfunctory. I made it clear that I did not relish the prospect of working full-time on civil defence, far away from the ordinary business of the Department. Was this the only way of employing someone refreshed by sabbatical leave? Was it not possible to contemplate a two-way or three-way move involving some other people?

In later years the personal preferences of civil servants in the Scottish Office about fields of work were to be given much more weight, but at that time the assumption was that the Department's view about where an individual was to be employed should be accepted without fuss. As the discussion went on, it was obvious that my arguments were making no impression, and since, partly in reaction to the almost off-hand way in which I had been told my fate, I was expressing them more forcibly than perhaps I should, I was succeeding only in making myself unpopular. Moreover, a little voice within kept telling me that if reinforcement was required someone presumably had to provide it; and it was the Establishment Officer's job to find him. I concluded that this was an encounter in which I was going to be the loser, and at the end of a somewhat testy exchange I accepted my fate with, I am afraid, an ill grace.

The salt mine was located well away from St. Andrew's House in a group of terraced houses in an unfashionable part of the New Town of Edinburgh. Since my last involvement with civil defence the goal posts had been moved. Instead of having to reckon with damage and casualties resulting from atomic bombs, we now had to assume greater devastation over larger areas of the country resulting from the much more powerful hydrogen bombs. But even if cities were destroyed, there would still be peripheral areas in which something could be done to deal with casualties and to maintain some sort of ordered existence. It was our job in association with local authorities, hospital boards, public utilities and voluntary bodies to draw up plans and make preparations for life, and death, after the bombs had dropped. There were some in the community who wanted the Government to 'ban the bomb' and desist from civil defence preparations, but they confined themselves to an occasional march with as much publicity as they could muster. In Scotland, at least, they did not mount any significant campaign by letter, deputation, or political pressure to persuade the Government to call an end to civil defence.

My assistant secretary colleague, Edward Elliot-Binns, had been in charge of the Department's one civil defence division for several years. Perhaps it was because he added service with the wartime SOS to the more conventional qualifications of an administrative civil servant that he seemed well cast for the job. He knew all the ins and outs of civil defence policy; he seemed completely at home in presenting doom and disaster and how to deal with them; and he knew everyone who mattered in civil defence in England as well as Scotland. If he thought it unnecessary and unsettling to have his empire cut in two, as well he might and probably did, he did not show it. I took from him responsibility for the branches dealing with the Civil Defence Corps and all questions concerning its recruitment and training in peace-time; medical services in war; and emergency supplies of food. He retained responsibility for, among other things, the planning of civil defence operations generally, including the structure of command and control. Where civil defence had to be dealt with as a single entity we were both involved; but in these contexts he inevitably had the leading role.

As the weeks went by I settled down to work in this untypical corner of the British bureaucracy. While the branch responsible for the Civil Defence Corps, a body of real people who actually met, trained and donned uniforms, had a good deal of conventional administrative work to do, the other branches were concerned primarily to devise plans on paper for situations often difficult to imagine. We had the inevitable office meetings to consider the possible shape of these plans. The head of the branch would then prepare a first draft; we would go over it together; perhaps an amended draft would be prepared; it would be sent to representatives of local authorities or hospital boards and later discussed with them; it might again be amended . . . and eventually some at least of these plans would be enshrined in official circulars.

I saw nothing at all of ministers during this period. It had been the Conservative Government of the early 1960s which had decided to intensify civil defence preparations, but having set the ball rolling they seemed content to let officials work away in what was an arid field ignored by the vast mass of the voters. I had arrived on the scene towards the end of that Government's life, and in October 1964 it was replaced by the first Labour Government for thirteen years. In their first year they had many other matters higher in their list of priorities to engage their interest and their energies, and we were left to carry on the good work as before.

I sat in splendour in what had once been a gracious drawing room. I had been astonished when I first arrived to find an open fire burning cheerfully. It was burning cheerfully each morning when I arrived at the office. A scuttle of coal sat alongside, but it was not for me to soil my hands keeping the fire stoked. From time to time a messenger would open the door, look at the fire, and if we thought it necessary would add a few well-chosen lumps to the flames. No other vestiges of earlier occupation remained. The furniture was standard civil service issue and included — most important for this job — a lockable filing cabinet. Many of the papers which came on my desk had not a whisper of secrecy about them — not surprising, as a major part of our job was to produce circulars for general distribution to public bodies. But there were always some which were 'classified', and they had to be carefully locked away when not in use. Concern about the consequences of nuclear attack was as nothing compared to the concern I sometimes felt on the way home at the end of the day about whether I had locked the cabinet. More than once I went back — and found that all was well.

I was happy to renew my acquaintance with Taymouth Castle. There members of the Civil Defence Corps were trained; there we organised courses and conferences for emergency food officers, medical superintendents of hospitals and other professional groups with a special role in war-time. Exposition to these various audiences of plans for dealing with death and destruction on a hitherto unimaginable scale became part of everyday life. If debate among the zealots became rather oppressive — even civil defence produced its enthusiasts for this, and diehard opponents of that — there were splendid therapeutic walks in the grounds, and there were trout to be persuaded from the River Tay. Sometimes too there were conferences at the Civil Defence Staff College at Sunningdale in Berkshire. There in a pleasant leafy Home Counties environment we discussed civil defence in a Great Britain rather than Scottish context not only with colleagues from London departments but also with representatives of public authorities from all parts of the UK. The extra-mural activities were not, however, as agreeable as those at Taymouth.

And so the salt-mine had its compensations. Important among the other compensations were my fellow miners, my colleagues. Very different in personality and style, my heads of branches were all congenial work-mates; and some official relationships born out of talk of blast and fall-out developed into life-long friendships. Most of us in the civil defence divisions were career civil servants; among those who were not, there were two ex-army men who added their special yeast to our mixture of experience. They could hardly have been more different from each other. Ian Buchanan-Dunlop, one of the heads of branch in the other division, was a retired Brigadier, quiet, courteous, a man of few words, who in his leisure time was a water-colourist of great skill and who later in retirement established an art gallery. Frank Richardson, a former Major-General in the RAMC, was an exuberant, boisterous character, a teller of tales, a bagpiper of great renown, an expert on the Peninsular War who wrote several books about Napoleon. I had more dealings with Frank, since he was our medical adviser. We seldom had a session with him which was not enlivened by gales of laughter. Discussion of arrangements for the collection of casualties would be punctuated not only by perceptive comments based on personal experience in the field of battle but also by reference to distantly related or even unrelated topics such as childbirth among the camp-followers of Wellington's army, the sex-life of Napoleon, or cavalry officers who were so stupid that even the other cavalry officers noticed it.

But in spite of all the compensations I never settled happily into civil defence work. When I visited St. Andrew's House canteen and heard the chat about policies and people in the other fields of more immediate public concern, I always felt out on a limb. The bush telegraph began to indicate that some new developments were in prospect in the health service divisions, as a result, it seemed, of pressure by the new Chief Medical Officer, John (later to become Sir John) Brotherston, former Professor of Public Health and Social Medicine at Edinburgh University. One day late in 1965 when I happened to encounter Brotherston, he volunteered, showing little sign of the inhibitions which governed those long steeped in civil service practice, that I would soon be doing something more interesting than civil defence.

Some weeks later all was officially revealed. There was to be set up in SHHD a Health Services Research and Intelligence Unit. The object was to have a group of people relieved of day to day administrative responsiblities who would be able to collect and analyse information about all aspects of the health service, study long-term trends, and provide those responsible for considering future policies with a sound factual basis for their consideration. It was also to circulate the information inside and outside the Department; to conduct research, other than medical research, into the working of the service; to stimulate others to do so; and to give financial support when this was thought appropriate. The unit was to be under the control of two joint directors — a principal medical officer and an assistant secretary. The principal medical officer was to be Dr Michael Heasman, the medical statistician from the Ministry of Health, and I was to be the assistant secretary.

In principle, this seemed all very enlightened, and the prospect of moving from civil defence made me content to jettison earlier hopes of entering some new field other than the NHS. The main job of the assistant secretary, I was told, apart from sharing the general management of the unit, was to be the link between the unit and the policy divisions, and to ensure that when it had produced reports they were fully considered and, it was to be hoped, implemented by the divisions concerned. Apart from that it was to see that the unit did not fly off into the stratosphere but concerned itself with practical problems. Kind words from John Brotherston and senior administrative officers about my experience of the health service and the contribution I could make to this new initiative made me suppress a certain scepticism about whether the role envisaged for the assistant secretary amounted to a full day's work. A remaining doubt about joint appointments and the possibilities they offered for uneasy working relationships was muted when I met Mike Heasman. Even if we did not always agree — and it was unlikely that we always would — I was sure we would be able amicably to resolve our differences of view and work together.

Like many another new development the unit was not entirely a new creation. We took over the Department's existing work study branch and the single existing research officer. Nonetheless, as higher authority, and in particular John Brotherston, insisted, the unit must be seen as something new with an identity of its own. To some extent it must be a free-standing entity with which people in the health service could identify and to which they could turn for advice and support. If this was to happen not only must there be additional staff, but the unit needed to be in its own building where it could show its own public face. A separate building was found — the old Simpson Maternity Hospital in Lauriston Place. This had been abandoned by the obstetricians and the midwives many years before for bright new premises along the road. If it still looked abandoned and run-down it was at least, so the argument went, an independent base for the unit which in due course could be transformed into a centre of enlightenment.

If an important part of my job was to liaise with and lean on the people in St. Andrew's House and ensure that they took full account of the work of the unit, I ought, it seemed to me, to have a room in St. Andrew's House. It is natural and only too easy for people responsible for running something to brush off or erect elaborate defences against gadfly organisations without responsibilities who seem to be telling them how to do their job. If I was seen to be part of the health service divisions and not a visiting representative from what might be seen as an upstart group from the other side of town, the unit would find it easier to make its mark on St. Andrew's House. In this honeymoon period everything was possible. I became the tenant of two rooms, one in St. Andrew's House, which became my main base, and the other at the old Simpson. This was a happy conjunction of good administrative sense and personal preference — for I welcomed a return to the headquarters building of the Scottish Office.

The principal task of the joint directors in the early days was to build up the unit and get it on the road. The grand official pronouncements about the role of the unit were not matched by any lavish budget. We could appoint only a very small number of additional doctors, research officers and other staff. But drawing up advertisements, sifting through applications, conducting interviews, and indoctrinating successful candidates took up a good deal of time. With something less than a handful of research officers we could start only a very few in-house research projects. Granted the complexity and scope of the NHS and all the possibilities for research into the workings of the many parts, it would never have been realistic to see the main role of the unit as trying to do research across the board at its own hand. More effective long-term results would flow from the promotion of research by other people and the encouragement throughout the service of the need to examine existing procedures and consider alternative methods. We made contact with key people in hospital boards, the hospitals themselves and university departments; we did what we could to encourage this approach and helped some people with studies of their own.

In so doing we had to take account of suggestions and pressures from John Brotherston, a strong and persistent character, known in some quarters as 'Big Brother'. When soon after our appointment he was laid low by an infection caught during a visit to the Middle East we were summoned to his home, there to be received by a grey-faced figure in pyjamas and dressing-gown determined to ensure that we were doing all the right things. In the weeks after his return to work ideas came flowing from him — ideas about research projects and the university departments which might be involved. Most of them we were happy to follow up along with ideas of our own. But we did not always see eye to eye. He welcomed discussion and debate; but since he combined the characteristics of the steam-roller and the terrier — and was, after all, our senior officer — he usually carried the day. We did have a few victories from time to time. But when he spoke for 45 minutes after having agreed to give an introductory talk of 15 minutes at a day conference we had arranged, we could only mutter silently to ourselves, pick up the pieces and re-cast the whole day's programme.

After a year or so the unit was well established, and it had become increasingly clear that while Mike was extremely busy I was not fully employed. The concept had always been that the two directors had different contributions to make. While we had each been involved in the build-up period, and in the continuing general management of the unit, I found that the role envisaged for me in linking the activities of the unit to the work of the administrative divisions did not amount to very much — largely because in the nature of research activity it was a long time before reports of studies began to appear and when they did appear they were few in number. Both of us participated in discussion with people in hospitals and universities, but it was for my colleague, a professional in the fields of medicine, statistics and research, rather than me, a general administrator, to get involved in the detail of projected studies. It was he, too, who was principally involved in that part of the unit's task which was to extend and improve the collection and publication of health statistics.

On earlier health service jobs I had always studied the *British Medical Journal* and the *Lancet* for news and comment on medical politics and the profession's attitude to Government policies. I had also enjoyed their less serious notes on *materia non medica*. Now, with no PQs, no ministerial correspondence and few dead-lines to meet, I found myself spending more time with these and other journals. As before, I passed over learned contributions about new surgical procedures or pathological investigations, but I read a good deal about epidemiology — the study of the incidence and prevalence of disease; and I became fascinated by some aspects of medical terminology. While many, if not most, medical conditions bore cool Latin-based names giving no hint of reality behind them, a few had labels which could hardly have been more dramatically descriptive. If 'fulminating beri-beri' was unlikely to be encountered by the average practitioner, 'strangulated hernia' was far from rare. Many diseases and syndromes bore the names of individuals who first identified and described them, e.g. Crohn's Disease; the Guillaume-Barre syndrome. Similarly the names of many tests, vaccines and procedures — e.g. the Wasserman test, the Salk vaccine, and pasteurisation (so much part of the language that the capital letter has disappeared) — were each a memorial to one man's inspiration, or inspiration combined with hard work, good luck or helpful colleagues. It was interesting to note how many of these were German or French. Did grateful patients, I wondered, know that they owed as much if not more to these and other medical scientists, and to the often criticised drug firms, as they did to the politicians who claimed so much credit for the National Health Service?

I had time also to reflect rather nostalgically on the days when as a busy young administrator I had set off from time to time on the night sleeper train to London. Sleeping one's way to and from the metropolis was, and probably still is, part of the way of life of most senior staff in the Scottish Office. The frequency of these visits varied according to the work on which one was engaged. For most people including myself an occasional visit every few weeks was a welcome change in the routine; too frequent visits were tiresome and disruptive. Some people — the Permanent Under Secretary of State, those busy with legislation before Parliament, and ministers' private secretaries — made a return journey every week when Parliament was sitting; and there were well authenticated tales of other individuals who had slept four nights in a row in sleepers. Now as I sat reading my journals, with no duties likely to take me to London, I thought of the love-hate relationship which we had with British Rail and their sleepers.

It had of course always been possible since the late 1940s to fly to and from London, and I remembered one or two laboured flights on old 32-seater Dakotas. But even when the Viscounts appeared and the service improved down the years, travel by sleeper had several advantages. After the proverbial hard day at the office the weary bureaucrat could spend a quiet evening at home and the night in bed, albeit not his own bed, arriving before breakfast in London in time for even the earliest morning meeting. Flying involved either an evening of movement to, in and from an aircraft with practically no time at home, or getting up early for the first morning flight with the very real possibility of not arriving in time for a morning meeting. And so most of us continued to rely on the sleepers at least for journeys south.

British Rail reserved for use by the Scottish Office a very small number of sleepers on the *Night Scotsman*. (Some Edinburgh citizens affected to believe that the Office had tenant's rights over much of the train.) Allocations were made in St. Andrew's House. The prudent official fixing a London meeting some time ahead did not rely on the 'Official List' as it was called. He booked his sleeper at the station as soon as he could like any member of the public. If all sleepers were booked and the waiting list was long, he could try the official list; and he might be lucky. But a place on the official list rested shakily on seniority, and there was always a danger that he would be moved summarily from the list if a more senior officer was suddenly summoned to the ministerial presence in

London. If this happened, other possibilities — cancellations, travel by day train, travel by air — were rapidly considered. If all else failed, and the time of the meeting could not be changed, he sat up all night. Fortunately, I was never reduced to such desperate straits.

Unlike some of my colleagues who needed little pills to induce oblivion, I seldom had difficulty in actually sleeping in sleepers. I had, of course, had a good deal of practice in my early days as a minister's private secretary. I found it helpful to relaxation that every sleeper was fitted in exactly the same way, apart from some being mirror-images of the others, so that on crossing the threshold one entered familiar territory — not like a strange room in a strange hotel. It was certainly quieter and more comfortable in berth No. 5 in the middle of the coach than in No. 1 or No. 10 over the wheels at the end. But I seldom found in practice this made much difference to what might be called the sleep induction interval — the time between switching out the light and dropping off. Nor was I much impressed by the arguments of those who thought that if the plug was not firmly in its place in the wash-basin more noise came up from the track through the waste pipe, and sleep was affected. All the same I made sure the waste pipe was plugged.

There were from time to time problems and resulting exasperation — when in winter the heating would not come on; when in summer it would not go off (why was it on at all in summer? To please the Americans, we were told); when windows would not close; when they would not open. Return journeys from London in high summer sometimes had another hazard. After sitting all day in hot sunshine in sidings outside King's Cross the sleepers were like ovens impossible to cool even with windows wide open as they trundled through the humid night air of south-east England.

The sleeper coaches of those days, of pre-war design, were replaced in the seventies by glossier coaches with a smoother ride and better ventilation. The old ones had, however, several useful features, and a certain charm which the replacements lacked — and still lack. There was a little box fixed to the wall for keeping keys and cash; nearby was a hook with a soft pad on the wall behind it on which the gentleman traveller could put his gold hunter watch; under the wash-basin was a fine old fashioned facility which could be used during the night as an alternative to donning coat and shoes and shuffling to the end of the corridor; and in the morning the tray borne in by the attendant had not only a pot of tea and biscuits but also a jug of hot water.

All the attendants were males of fairly mature years and most of them had shuttled north and south on the sleepers for many years. They knew and were known by most of the regular passengers. The tale was told of one new recruit who was unsure what to do when one of his passengers, a gentleman in late middle age, became ill during the night complaining of severe pains in the chest. He consulted his colleague, an old stager, in the next coach. That worthy looked down the passenger list to see who might help. 'Dr A; he's no good, he's an obstetrician. Dr B; even worse, he's in social medicine. Ah! Dr C; he's a cardiologist, Let's wake him up.'

Of the occasional dramas of this kind, most passengers were quite unaware. Very occasionally, we were all too aware of awkward delays resulting from severe weather or re-routeing of trains because of problems on the track. But on the whole travel by sleeper was a routine and uneventful part of the official life. If anyone had an encounter in the middle of the night with a beautiful spy who thought she was on the Orient Express he never told his colleagues.

Meantime, my only train journeys were occasional sorties with Mike Heasman to Glasgow, Aberdeen or Dundee. While the work I was doing was agreeable enough, and Mike was a very congenial colleague, I was increasingly concerned about my under-employment. The sensible employee in such circumstances' should ask himself whether he is failing to see things which ought to be done or which can usefully be done, and whether he is failing to bring forth bright and original ideas which he or others might follow up. Even the most self-critical may sometimes find these difficult questions to answer. Is there not nearly always something more that might be done or thought up? Might it not sometimes however be a work of supererogation making no real contribution to the public weal? Trying to be as objective and self-critical as possible I concluded that anything more I might usefully be doing still did not make up a full time job for an assistant secretary. If my official conscience was reasonably clear in that respect, I was still concerned that the taxpayer was not getting full value for my salary. There was another, perhaps more pressing, consideration. Although not plagued by more than the average share of ambition, I hoped to climb higher in the hierarchy. At present I was doing little, and indeed was not in a very good position, to demonstrate my fitness for elevation.

Consultation with Mike Heasman and senior officers met with a sympathetic response. Though no one went as far as actually admitting that it had been an error to appoint an assistant secretary as full-time joint director of the Research and Intelligence Unit, there was acceptance of my suggestion that while remaining part-time director I should have other duties in addition. Within a few months I had no complaints about lack of work.

The first new responsibility to come my way was Foods Branch. This branch had been set up in pre-NHS days when most of the Department's health responsibility had lain in the field of environmental health and the control of infection. This responsibility continued after 1948 though rather overshadowed by the much larger responsibility for providing health care. Foods Branch had a wide range of culinary concerns — from the safety of milk to conditions in food shops: from the management of slaughterhouses to the contents of meat pies. The Secretary of State made Regulations drafted in the Department after consultation with interested bodies, on these and other matters under the Food and Drugs Acts. While it was for local health authorities to ensure that the Regulations were observed, it was for the Department to exhort and supervise the authorities. There was a battery of advisory committees, some covering the whole of Great Britain, some for Scotland alone. While questions of nutrition and the medical implications of what they ate and drank concerned Scots and English alike, there were produced in different parts of the United Kingdom various local delicacies much appreciated by those living in the area but sometimes viewed with suspicion by the unenlightened elsewhere. A separate Scottish health department would have been failing in its duty if it had not ensured that much favoured Scotch pies, bridies and sausages, not to mention haggis, were considered sympathetically.

I had for long remembered one incident from my early days in the Department. The assistant secretary then in charge of Foods Branch had burst into a room in which I and others were sitting, his eyes popping, his hands holding an ancient file which he had come across in some forgotten recess. The title on the file was 'Rats' tails, cats' tails [and something else which, perhaps mercifully, I have forgotten] for stiffening up jujubes'. The files which came to me from Foods Branch never conjured up such macabre prospects. And since in the late sixties the proper public concern about the contents and safety of food did not amount to the hysteria which so often erupted in the late eighties, the work of the branch never hit the front pages of the public prints.

Along with responsibility for the Foods Branch, I also assumed — co-incidentally, be it emphasised — responsibility for burials and cremations. Following the work of the Broderick Committee on that subject, the Government was considering legislation to implement at least some of its recommendations. But the subject was not one which greatly excited politicians or public; there were more pressing demands on legislators' time; and nothing much happened. All that I was called to do under the heading was to sign from time to time on behalf of the Secretary of State a formal document authorising the cremation in Scotland of someone who had died abroad while on holiday. In such circumstances it was impossible to follow all the normal procedures carried out when people die in this country, and a special authorisation was required. The first time such a document appeared on my desk for signature, accompanied by a batch of papers, some of the originals in Italian, I was slightly shaken by what seemed to be an awesome responsibility. But the branch was used to this growing traffic; they had devised appropriate procedures for dealing with it, and seemed to have done their work well. All I had to do, I was told, was to sign my name. Since cremation is a very final act, more final than burial, I took my time. It was easier on the next and subsequent occasions.

Soon I was given a more substantial, potentially a much more substantial, block of work.

The NHS, now almost twenty years old, was a well established part of the fabric of British life. It was accepted by all political parties, the professions and the public as a Good Thing, by no means beyond improvement here and there, but not needing fundamental change. Comparisons with the prosperous society of the United States of America only confirmed the general view that what was on offer here was a much better deal for the vast mass of the citizens. Without showing much sign of knowledge of what was available elsewhere, some politicians went as far as describing the NHS as the best health service in the world. Those actually running the service had, however, become increasingly aware that its administrative structure was cumbrous in some respects, and some tentative consideration had been given in the Health Departments to changes which would both reduce the administrative complexity and provide a more efficient service. While ministers knew that this work was in hand and were content that it should continue, they showed no eagerness to embark on a major reform which would involve legislation — legislation which would deal only with what might be portrayed as tedious administrative matters not directly affecting the service provided for the citizens. Nonetheless, the work was likely to increase, and I was given responsibility for coordinating our departmental effort.

The basic problem was that the administrative structure of the NHS when established in 1948 consisted of three separate parts. There were hospital boards responsible for hospital and specialist services; executive councils, which made available the services of general practitioners, dentists, pharmacists and opticians; and local health authorities, that is, the larger councils of local government, which dealt with public health, increasingly known as environmental health, and the control of infection in the community. So far as hospitals were concerned, there was a further complication; regional hospital boards planned services over fairly wide areas while under them separate boards of management ran individual hospitals or groups of hospitals. All this meant that in any one part of the country there were at least three authorities providing health services; and there was no one authority responsible for the general planning and provision of health care for the whole population of the area. It was not the job of the central government department to coordinate the services on the ground but sometimes, willy-nilly, it found itself doing exactly that. On the whole, the system worked much better than this bald description of the structure might suggest. Professional people working in the different parts of the service — general practitioners and specialists, for example — had their own lines of communication, and there was no evidence that the treatment of individual patients was adversely affected. But general opinion in the departments at least was that with some radical changes the whole system could be made to work effectively, especially in the planning of future provision.

I took over what was already a fairly thick file of papers consisting mainly of thoughts and ideas exchanged by senior officials in the Health Departments. It was generally agreed that the tripartite service had had its day and should be replaced by a unitary structure. But there were many particular questions which needed further study. I got down to considering some of these with colleagues, senior and junior, professional and administrative in the time-honoured way. We had office meetings; we identified the problems, possible changes and objections to them; papers were written by me and others; we began to reach some conclusions. We kept in touch with the Ministry of Health and its successor the Department of Health and Social Security — though the different scale of the operation in the two countries almost certainly meant that different types of new organisational structures would be needed. But what would be the use of all this activity and all the ideas which we generated if ministers remained reluctant to move?

There are many reasons apart from the contents of party programmes why things happen or do not happen in government. Sometimes it is clear to everyone that something has to be done, and it is done. Sometimes there is pressure difficult to resist. But sound arguments are not enough. When there is no compelling need for change sound arguments, even if widely accepted, may not be sufficient to outweigh the trouble and disruption inevitably caused by change. It is in these circumstances that ministerial will, or the absence of it, is significant. I was never clear why in relation to health service reorganisation ministers who had been reluctant to move quite suddenly decided that they should act. True, in the traditional style of all British Governments in these careful pre-Thatcher days, they announced late in 1967 merely an intention to review the administrative structures of the service, consulting, informally at first, the interested bodies. But this changed the whole climate, and work on NHS reorganisation had a new urgency.

We set up several informal working groups containing representatives of the Department, the health service bodies and the professions to study the implications of administrative change and what form it might take. These groups were to be a means by which the Department tested opinion before drawing up proposals for more general, formal, consideration. We sat through many long afternoons during which all sorts of notions were advanced, considered, discarded, amended, and even accepted. John Brotherston, that constant source of radical ideas, took a leading role. He believed with some justification that only if there were administrative changes could doctors, some at present responsible to one body and some to another, so organise themselves, their training and their ideas for the future of medicine that the best possible service to patients generally could be planned and delivered. Not everyone agreed with all his proposals and some of his ideas fell on stony ground. But he was a force to be reckoned with.

It was agreed with ministers that in the light of these discussions we in the Department would draft a 'Green Paper'. Green Papers were now very much in vogue. Until the 1960s, governments had set out their proposals in White Papers. These by convention were usually proposals to which they were fairly firmly, though not irrevocably, committed. Increasingly, there had been felt a need for a type of paper which set out ideas and proposals to which the government was by no means committed, but which they thought deserved consideration. Such were Green Papers. Our Green Paper would commit none of the outside members of the working groups, and they like anyone else would be free to comment and criticise. With John Walker, the principal who worked with me on the exercise, I prepared the first draft of the Green Paper. It was circulated, discussed and amended in the Department. It was accepted by the Secretary of State, Mr William Ross (known universally in homely style, in spite of his fierce and prickly personality, as Willie Ross). It was published in December 1968, and all and sundry were invited to let us have their views on its proposals.

The main proposal was that in place of all the multifarious hospital boards, executive councils and local health authorities there should be appointed a number, somewhere between 10 and 15, of area health boards. Each board, to be appointed by the Secretary of State, would be responsible for the planning and the day-to-day management of nearly all the health services in its area. There would be, in addition, a new central body, which would be responsible for providing those services, such as the ambulance service, which because of their nature were best provided on an all-Scotland basis. This body would also provide some common services, e.g. legal services and supplies services, for health boards; and the Department would shed to it those activities such as the Research and Intelligence Unit which did not need to belong to the Secretary of State's central policy-making department. All sorts of detailed implications were considered — the size of the boards, the areas to be covered, staff, buildings, and many others.

It did not take the interested bodies long to address themselves to the proposals in this Green Paper, and as the months of 1968 went by reactions kept coming in. There was no doubt about the general acceptance of the basic proposition that a unitary structure with one board for each area should replace the tripartite structure. But what the boundaries of the areas should be; what functions should be given to the new central agency — on these and other matters views differed. Happily they did not differ so fundamentally or so strongly as to make it unlikely that we could devise a detailed new structure which would command fairly general assent.

Suddenly out of the blue there came a new development. Ronald Johnson, Secretary of the Department, told me he proposed to nominate me to the Civil Service Department for the post of head of the Edinburgh Centre of the soon to be established Civil Service College. It seemed that one chapter of my official career might be about to come to an end and another begin.

Chapter 9

Civil Service College

Early in 1966 Mr Harold Wilson's Government had set up a committee with Lord Fulton in the chair 'to examine the structure, recruitment and management, including training, of the Home Civil Service, and to make recommendations'. That was not in itself a very bold or radical step. Down the years there had been many committees reviewing the Civil Service, and only ten years before, another committee, a Royal Commission no less, appointed by a Conservative Government, had produced a report of 238 pages. But the Wilson Government was eager to make changes in British society; it was anxious to reap the social and economic benefits of what it called the white heat of the technological revolution; and some at least of its members doubted whether the Civil Service, by its composition, structure and methods of working, was able to give it the support it needed. While the terms of reference were neutral enough, and the members seemed a reasonably balanced selection from the ranks of what in the trade are known as the Great and the Good, the Government no doubt hoped that the left-wingers on the committee — and Lord Fulton himself inclined in that direction — would ensure the production of a radical and far-reaching report.

Reviews of the Civil Service, whatever their origin or purpose, are never likely to be unpopular. There are some on the left for whom it is an article of faith that the Civil Service, reactionary and élitist at least in the higher ranks, would frustrate the plans of a left wing government or sabotage the implementation of its legislation. Some on the right are convinced that the Civil Service must be a second-rate organisation, since anyone with drive and ability would prefer to be out in the competitive world creating new business and making money. The press, in love for the most part with its stereotypes, tends to see civil servants as slow, over-cautious, lacking the lively imaginative qualities of the journalist, and very much in need of a good shake-up. Echoes of all these views must have been in the minds of many of those individuals and organisations who diligently submitted views and information to Lord Fulton and his colleagues.

The Committee's report, published in June 1968, contained 158 recommendations, some indeed radical and far-reaching. Apart from the recommendations, which do not concern us here, for changes in the structure of the Civil Service — by no means all of which were implemented — there were two major recommendations which were put into effect very quickly, and which were soon to alter the course of my career. The first was that a new government department, the Civil Service Department, should be created to take over the management and control of the Civil Service from the Treasury. The second was that a Civil Service College should be established to provide major courses in administration and management. The College should have two centres — a residential centre reasonably close to London and a non-residential centre in London itself. Governments are not in the habit of going the extra mile; but after considering all the implications of the Fulton Report, the Wilson Government decided that a college of three parts, not two, was required. The third centre should be somewhere in the north well away from London. Possible sites, which had to be close to the teaching resources of a university, were investigated; and in the summer of 1969 it was announced that the third centre of the College would be established in Edinburgh. It would take over premises soon to be vacated by the Edinburgh College of Domestic Science for which new accommodation was under construction in a western suburb.

All this was only vaguely in my mind when the Secretary of SHHD told me he was proposing to nominate me for the post of head of the Edinburgh centre. The post was to be at assistant secretary level and therefore no promotion was involved; but an allowance, by no means derisory, was to be paid in recognition of the unusual nature of the responsibilities. The period of tenure was not fixed, but several years were certainly in mind. To me, this seemed a pretty clear indication that there was no early prospect of promotion in the Scottish Office. If I had been regarded as one of the highest of the fliers destined for one of the topmost posts, I would by now, aged 46 and with nine years seniority as an assistant secretary, have been knocking on the door, or even through the door and sitting in an under secretary's chair. Had the various jobs, unsatisfactory as they seemed to me, which I had been given since my return from sabbatical leave contributed to this failure to impress? Would the results have been the same if I had been in some mainstream, more demanding, assistant secretary post? There was no means of knowing, and there was little point in speculation. This new possibility would again take me away from mainstream administrative activity. But the prospect of having a leading role in the establishment of a new organisation was attractive; and good conduct in posts with allowances led more often than not to eventual promotion. And so with modified rapture, I said I would be glad to be nominated.

That in itself did not ensure me the job. I do not know how many departments made nominations or how many nominees were interviewed; but some weeks later I appeared before two senior officers of the Civil Service Department (now known generally as the CSD). One was Hugh Taylor, an old Admiralty hand who had just been appointed Deputy Principal of the College. We had a talk rather than an interview in which my ideas about the Civil Service and Civil Service training were sought and discussed. I do not know whether these ideas would have been regarded as enlightened and forward-looking by the more radical critics of the Civil Service, but they must have satisfied my two interlocutors. I had hardly entered the office back in Edinburgh before I heard that I was appointed.

On 1st November 1969 I was formally seconded from the Scottish Office to the CSD to act as head of the Edinburgh Centre of the yet to be born Civil Service College. The premises of the College of Domestic Science were still occupied by young ladies busily making cakes, doing the laundry and learning about institutional management. I had nowhere to go. With my secretary Jeanette Wallace, who had chosen to accompany me, I had to stay for the present in St. Andrew's House.

Planning for the new College was going on apace in CSD, and once more I became a regular traveller to London. There I met another visitor from northern parts — Professor Eugene Grebenik of Leeds University who had just been appointed Principal-Designate of the College. I attended the first of many meetings with Grebbie, as he was known at Leeds and came to be known in CSD, and senior staff of the Training and Education Division of the Treasury, whose responsibilities for providing central training would be taken over by the College. As I looked across at Grebbie, I wondered whether those responsible for appointing the Principal had decided to spike the guns of those critics who were obsessed by the supposed élitism of the Civil Service by looking for someone who, while of good academic standing, had none of the characteristics so often attributed to the archetypical senior civil servant. If so,

Grebbie certainly seemed to fill the bill. His accent did not proclaim a privileged background and attendance at an expensive English public school. He had in fact a slight foreign accent, and had been educated abroad. Too many civil servants in the view of the critics had studied medieval history, Latin or subjects irrelevant to the needs of the twentieth century. Grebbie was a professor of social studies. What could be more relevant? He did not come from the pampered colleges of Oxford or Cambridge: a man from Leeds might be expected to bring with him a practical northern grittiness. At the first meeting, however, northern grittiness was not much in evidence. It was an urbane exchange in which facts, arguments and ideas were tossed to and fro — rather like a tutorial of the better sort, except that it was not obvious who was the tutor and who the tutored.

Another person I met — or rather, to whose presence I was summoned — on one of these early London visits was Sir William Armstrong, Permanent Secretary of the CSD and Head of the Civil Service. Armstrong had been seen and heard in public more than most of his predecessors. He had appeared frequently on television, and the more popular newspapers had lightened dreary news items about the Civil Service during the post-Fulton debates by telling the readers again and yet again that the Head of the Civil Service was the son of Salvation Army Officers. I was therefore prepared to meet a familiar figure, modest in demeanour and quietly authoritative in speech.

When I appeared at the appointed hour the figure I encountered was not quite as I had visualised. It was not only that he sat in shirt sleeves and braces rather than conventional jacket, or that he was wrapped in cigarette smoke. The face seemed tired and worn, and there was an air of sadness about him. True, the day was far spent; no doubt he had been very busy, and perhaps there was still much to be done. But he began to talk about the College and his ideas about Civil Service training as if they were the only things on his mind. Edinburgh must become just as important a part of the College as the two other centres in the south. The division of labour between the three centres must be functional not geographical; there was no question of Edinburgh dealing only, or even primarily, with people from Scotland and the North of England. If geography were to be a significant factor there might be a case for sending everyone from the south to Edinburgh, and vice versa, so that they could see how the other half lived. But that was not practical. What was important was that each centre should provide a range of courses, and civil servants should go to whichever centre provided the course they needed. At appropriate points I answered a question or volunteered a comment. There seemed to be no urgency to terminate the interview; but eventually he rose, rather wearily, and wished me well.

During the winter there were many meetings in London with Grebbie, Hugh Taylor and others who were to become senior staff of the College. With the shadow of Fulton never far away, we considered the role of the College and how that differed from the training now given in departments. Clearly, it was for the Inland Revenue and DHSS to continue to guide their big battalions through the complexities of taxation and national insurance; and other departments too had their special areas of responsibility about which they had to do their own indoctrination. Apart from that, all departments must continue to provide some training of a more general kind in management and organisation. It was for the College to provide central training for the groups specially mentioned by Fulton — graduates recruited to what had formerly been called the Administrative Class (now sunk, though not without trace, in what was now a classless but by no means grade-less Civil Service); specialists such as architects, scientists and economists entering the professional grades and needing training in administration and mangement; and selected people in other grades likely to move up to posts of greater responsibility. No doubt other needs would appear before long. The College would provide training (or was it education?) in economics, statistics, personnel management, the structure of government and the use of computers — the actual content of the courses being determined by the needs of the particular group for whom they were intended. We turned to the practical questions of accommodation, staff and courses.

Accommodation did not take us long at that stage. It had already been decided where the two residential centres would be. The former Civil Defence Staff College at Sunningdale Park, now used by the Treasury for courses for civil servants, would become the College's residential centre near London. It was already well suited for the purpose. It consisted of a splendid 1930s country mansion deep in stockbroker country which had come into the ownership of the Crown, and of blocks of residential accommodation recently constructed among the pines on the estate. The Edinburgh centre had to be adapted in ways yet to be determined; but for the present that was left for me to consider with the Ministry of Public Buildings and Works (MPBW) in Edinburgh. Negotiations were in hand for property in Belgrave Road to be used as the non-residential centre in London.

Staffing was important, and probably more important than premises, if the college was to become an institution of some distinction and not merely a treadmill providing routine courses. The intellectual level of the teaching in economics and other academic disciplines had to be high, but not so elevated as to part company completely with the day to day problems faced by staff at different levels in government departments. There would be two groups of staff. First, directors of programmes, normally civil servants, who would be responsible for planning and organising courses for particular groups, and under them course directors, again civil servants, who would run individual courses. Second, there would be directors of studies in, for example, statistics, economics and personnel management, recruited from the universities, who would be responsible for the academic content of the courses; under them there would be a number of full time lecturers. In addition, other lecturers and tutors — academics, serving civil servants and people from industry and commerce — would be employed *ad hoc*.

In our first division of labour between the centres Edinburgh was allocated courses for two main groups — the professionals and specialists needing training in administration and management, and middle managers in the Executive grades expected to move to more senior posts. Other courses would follow. When we could begin this training would depend on when we could get access to the premises, and on the service we could get from our colleagues in the MPBW, a group who always did a good job but whose speed of delivery sometimes failed to impress their customers in other departments.

One staffing question close to home, an important question for me personally, was the appointment of my deputy at the Edinburgh centre. It had been visualised from the outset that while the head of the centre need not be an expert in training, he should have a second-in-command with experience of organising courses for civil servants. This was an arrangement with which I thoroughly agreed as I had no experience of translating concepts into curricula, far less actually running courses. Among the training staff of the CSD whom I met in the early days was K.J. Shanahan, known to one and all as Shan, an Australian who had come to Britain during the war and had never gone back. His experience of departmental training in the old Ministry of Pensions and National Insurance and central training in the Treasury made him ideally suited for the job. I had already come to enjoy his lively incisive turn of phrase and his store of comments and aphorisms, some original, others too good not to be given an occasional airing. I was later to appreciate exactly what he meant when he described one junior colleague as a good man to help you get out of trouble he should never have got you into in the first place. Shan was appointed deputy head of the Edinburgh centre.

In Edinburgh immediately after my appointment I had paid my first visit to the buildings to be vacated by the College of Domestic Science. I was not particularly impressed. The College property consisted mainly of three blocks of accommodation in what had been an elegant early nineteenth century crescent of terraced houses in the western part of the New Town — numbers 1–8, number 12 and most of numbers 15–17 Atholl Crescent. There was no intercommunication between these three parts of the establishment, and such elegance as now remained was all for the external beholder. The headquarters of the College were in numbers 1–8. On the ground, basement and first floors there was teaching and administrative accommodation; the upper floors contained residential accommodation for students. In what had been the gardens at the back there was a gimcrack collection of wooden buildings containing demonstration kitchens and teaching equipment of varying antiquity. No wonder, I thought, the College was moving out. There was a run-down air about the whole place which was, I supposed, the effect as well as the cause of the decision to move. I hoped the MPBW could make something of all this; they, after all, had been parties to the decision to take it over.

My spirits rose when I saw two other buildings nearby owned by the College and used as residences. One of these, Melvin House in Rothesay Terrace, had been the home of John Ritchie Findlay, a nineteenth century owner and editor of the *Scotsman* newspaper. Impressive enough from the outside, it was positively sumptuous inside, with a fine marble staircase, a spacious drawing room and a library in the grand manner complete with balcony and spiral staircase. On the upper floors were single bedrooms created out of accommodation designed for the days of large families and large staffs. It did not take me long to decide that whatever the problems of adapting the Atholl Crescent premises, Melvin House was ideally suited to provide teaching accommodation for about forty students, and residential accommodation for more than half of them. Not all the splendour of the public rooms, of the fascinating detail of the woodwork and brasswork (even the brass key-hole covers bore the initials J.R.F.) could mask the inadequacy of the kitchen, the impoverishment of the heating system and the need for improvement of the bedrooms. But these were modest adaptations compared to what seemed required at Atholl Crescent itself.

I made contact with the staff of the Scottish headquarters of the MPBW, the first of a series of consultations with their administrators, architects, surveyors and engineers which were to go on during my whole period at the Civil Service College. Although the College of Domestic Science was not to vacate the premises completely until the end of the current session we could get access to numbers 15–17 before that. We decided to plan for the early conversion of that part of the property and its use for the training of civil servants from the autumn of 1970.

Meanwhile, there was a more immediate accommodation problem. I could not stay for long in St. Andrew's House; Shan would soon be joining me, and other staff would soon be appointed. We had to find somewhere to park ourselves. Fortunately, there was a vacant small office building not far off. One winter day Jeanette Wallace and I moved in. Soon we were joined by Shan. If the Edinburgh Centre of the Civil Service College was not yet a going concern, it was now in an active state of gestation.

As I have noted elsewhere, the planning of new buildings and the adaptation of premises is not my favourite form of administrative activity. When, however, the buildings are to be occupied by oneself, one's staff and one's students, it concentrates the mind wonderfully.

We had many hours of discussion with the MPBW and their consultant architects about each part of our premises in turn. At the end of many of these discussions the architects had to go back to the drawing board, to amend, adjust or even to start again. But there came the day when the last plans for a particular block were agreed and the men from the Ministry went off to deal with contractors. When the builders finished with the first block, numbers 15–17 Atholl Crescent, in the autumn of 1970, we admitted the first group of students and moved in ourselves. There was a formal opening by Lady Tweedsmuir, Minister of State at the Scottish Office. At last we were in business.

Edinburgh was a residential centre and we had to provide not only teaching accommodation but living accommodation for students. Before we had sufficient residential places of our own we used hotels, university hostels (when they were available) and even for a time part of the outbuildings of Holyrood Palace, premises used to accommodate staff of the Royal Household when the Queen was in residence. For a time too we used the bedrooms in the upper floors of 1–8 Atholl Crescent with only minor adaptation; but the erratic performance of the heating and lighting systems and fears about fire made us abandon these rooms to the ghosts of young ladies in white overalls.

Consideration of what should be the long term use of that building had been deferred while discussions went on in London about the future of the College as a whole. Shan and I had been going regularly to London and happily taking part in the regular Directors' Meetings about major College policy involving the Sunningdale and London centres as well as Edinburgh. On the other hand we were content not to be too closely involved in the detailed arrangements, which, it turned out, raised all sorts of delicate problems, for the formal opening of the College.

This, we had all decided, should take place at Sunningdale, the headquarters of the College, sometime in the summer of 1970. Thereafter, Grebbie, Hugh Taylor and our Sunningdale colleagues turned parts of their minds from educational philosophy to the higher forms of administrative mechanics. After negotiations with the Prime Minister's Office it was decided that Mr Harold Wilson would formally open the College on 26th June. All the usual complicated arrangements for such a high-powered occasion were well advanced when the same Mr Wilson decided to hold a General Election on 18th June. The drafting of the invitation cards was prudently revised to announce only that the opening would be performed by the 'Prime Minister'. In the event, by the evening of 18th June it was clear that on 26th June the Prime Minister would be Mr Edward Heath. Mr Heath in the next few days no doubt had many more important matters on his mind, but he agreed to open the College and address those who were expecting the 'Prime Minister' to appear.

26th June was a fine summer day. The grounds of Sunningdale looked marvellous. Grebbie and Hugh Taylor, on the other hand, looked slightly anxious as all the great ones gathered — Sir William Armstrong, Lord Jellicoe (Lord Privy Seal and Head of the Civil Service Department), and many others — and awaited the arrival of the Prime Minister for what was his first public duty in that office. I was in small group of people lined up to be introduced to the Prime Minister. When Mr Heath arrived he was duly introduced to those on my right, and then Grebbie introduced Mr Hume 'from Scotland', head of the Edinburgh Centre. Mr Heath immediately bridled. 'No one told me there would be anyone from Scotland,' he said to Grebbie in a thoroughly ill-tempered way. To me he offered his hand but not a word or a glance. I wondered why he was so put out. Did shaking the hand of someone from Scotland require special briefing or perhaps some kind of health warning? Down the years I had been accustomed to seeing in the House or on television Ted Heath of the toothy smile, the heaving shoulders and the hearty manner. Why now so abrasive — on a matter of no importance whatever? Strange man, I thought. But thereafter all went smoothly. The College was duly opened; we all had tea; and soon everyone including Mr Heath had departed to resume the business of government.

As one Directors' Meeting succeeded another, College activities increased and long-term plans for the future were agreed. Edinburgh, it was decided, should provide 400 places out of a College total of 1000. To achieve this aim we would need to make the most effective use of Nos. 1–8 Atholl Crescent, the largest part of our premises. What should we do with the wooden buildings at the back? One winter afternoon, a group of us, cold and depressed, completed another inspection of the sad and seedy collection of huts. 'The best thing to do with all this,' someone said, 'is to put a match to it.' And so, in a figurative sense at least, it was agreed. They would all be swept away; in their place we would build a residential block connected to the main building, and a fine College headquarters would result. Feasibility studies were started and a great deal of work was done. But by the time firm proposals were agreed the first careless post-Fulton rapture about Civil Service training was beginning to fade. The CSD and the Treasury were looking harder at costs and numbers. Our proposals had to be revised. And so it went on. Even when I left the College in the autumn of 1973 the ghosts still occupied Nos 1–8 and the horrors in the garden.

Meanwhile as the contractors completed their work on other parts of the empire, we were glad to see that what we had visualised when looking at plans did indeed provide pleasing and practical teaching and living accommodation. By mid-1972 there was accommodation for over 200 students. We had regular courses for young specialists, for middle managers in the executive grades and for people specialising in certain types of automatic data processing. In addition to this staple diet, we had from time to time seminars for senior civil servants — and some other people from outside the service — on topics of current interest and concern; and there were several courses on the EEC — how it was organised, how it functioned and what were its implications for the United Kingdom.

The Prime Minister was eager that as part of Britain's increasing links with European countries there should be exchange visits of civil servants. It was arranged that the College would from time to time organise courses for foreign civil servants, especially French and German, and there would be similar visits to Paris and Bonn by British civil servants. As a result of temporary accommodation problems in London and Sunningdale, Grebbie asked me whether one of the first visiting groups, a group from Bonn, could come to Edinburgh for a few days — the implication being that I would not be troubled again. We arranged to accommodate them in Melvin House and to organise a short programme of lectures and discussions. The Germans were so delighted with what was offered during their stay in the capital of Scotland — including the excursion which we organised into the interior of this intriguing land — that the German Civil Service College asked that all future German groups visiting the UK should similarly spend part of their time in Edinburgh. And so they did. And not only the Germans; the French as well. It was nice to have such satisfied customers.

To run a residential college for these different kinds of courses and groups we had to employ not only teaching staff but administrative, catering and housekeeping staff. The recruitment of teaching staff, as well as being the most important, was the most difficult. Well-qualified graduates looking for employment in higher education did not fall over themselves to apply for jobs in our untried institution with no established reputation in the academic world when there were attractive opportunities elsewhere. It had never been our intention that all teaching in the academic subjects should be done by the College's own lecturers, but it was not easy to attract as many full time staff as we would have liked. Academics from Colleges and Universities, if sceptical about the College as a full time employer, were, however, relatively easy to attract as visiting lecturers. The rates of pay we offered for lecture sessions were no doubt a welcome addition to their take-home pay. Other visiting lecturers came from local government, nationalised industries and business. A small number of civil servants were recruited as course directors, and others left their desks in their departments from time to time to talk about the business of government.

If some of my work as head of the centre was not far removed from conventional administrative work in a government department — for example, the planning of buildings, and the appointment and supervision of staff — much of it was very different. A residential college is a community, and inevitably the head by what he does, and what he does not do, helps to shape the character of that community for good or ill. This is done in various ways — by such rules as are laid down, by such conventions as are nurtured, and by the atmosphere which is generated. Contacts with staff were regular and frequent; much less so with students. Though I welcomed members of each course on their first day, dropped in from time to time during discussions, and had informal encounters over coffee and lunch, it was impossible to meet more than a small proportion of those who came to us from government offices, laboratories and research establishments all over Great Britain.

Sometimes the closest and most relaxed encounters took place at our College dinners on the last evening of each course. On these occasions we always had a visiting speaker, a senior figure from the world of government or someone whose work brought him into contact with the Civil Service. There was a blend

123

of formality and informality, and a convivial atmosphere was encouraged by the excellent fare offered by our catering staff. It was these regular opportunities to show professional skill at a level well above that of even good institutional cuisine that had enabled us to recruit and retain a team of excellent chefs. I sometimes thought that while it was difficult to know whether we ran a good college, there was no doubt on these occasions at least that we ran a good restaurant.

From the earliest days we had a regular stream of visitors eager to see how the centre was developing. It was inevitably part of my job to receive as many of them as possible, and not only to show them round, to explain, to listen, and to discuss, but also to entertain them. There was a roll call of knights from the CSD and other departments — Sir William Armstrong, Sir Ian Bancroft, Sir David Pitblado, and Sir Douglas Haddow among them. There were also the soon-to-be-knighted — like Nick Morrison of the CSD who succeeded Sir Douglas Haddow as Permanent Under Secretary of State at the Scottish Office. And there were others not so exalted but important enough to require the full treatment from the head of the Centre. Even CSD ministers ventured into our northern fastness. One after another they came — Paul Channon (the most distant), Kenneth Baker (the smoothest), Lord Jellicoe (the most genial) — and it seemed at times that name-dropping was part of our way of life. With Lord Jellicoe, we spent a specially entertaining afternoon. Before he left he had tea with the senior staff of the Centre. The catering staff had excelled themselves and Lord Jellicoe did full justice to what was on offer. As he left he thanked us for a splendid afternoon and 'an absolutely spiffing tea'.

Some interesting extra-mural activities came my way. On one occasion I went with Grebbie to an international conference in Brussels concerned with Civil Service training and education. Most of the countries of western Europe were represented. The conference itself was interesting enough, but what remains particularly in my mind was one encounter which did not take place. My senior colleague, who did not like formal occasions, decided that we should stay at the official evening reception only long enough to register our presence. Little did he know that soon after our departure the King of Belgium in his informal way arrived to circulate among conference delegates. Next morning I was greeted by the conference organiser with the unforgettable words: 'Ah, Mr Hume; where were you and Mr Grebenik yesterday evening? The King was looking for you.' I put together some words which I hoped would explain our early departure, and wondered how seriously the Belgians regarded the offence of *lèse-majesté*. Happily, they seemed to be amused rather than affronted. At any rate, I reflected, it was not every day that I was told a real live King had been looking for me.

That was not my only visit to Brussels on behalf of the CSD. Soon after I had joined the Department I had been appointed British representative on the Public Administration Committee of Western European Union. I had hardly heard of Western European Union, a rather shadowy body consisting of the Benelux countries, France, West Germany, Italy and Britain, whose primary role was to coordinate their defence and foreign policies. It had earlier had committees concerned with other subjects, but there remained now only its Public Administration Committee. This Committee, I gathered, was a forum of the exchange of information about Civil Service organisation and training; and it arranged various exchanges and courses for civil servants from member countries. The current British representative was leaving the CSD and I was asked to succeed him. I never asked, 'Why me?', a man from one of the outposts of the Department, as I welcomed this extension of my field of interest and the promised twice yearly trips abroad. Certainly I spoke some French, which was the only qualification about which my seniors seemed concerned; but the mystery remained.

I attended my first meeting of the Committee in the autumn of 1971 in Brussels. Every committee has its own ethos and persona to which the newcomer has to adapt; and I had not before joined a committee of which each member was of a different nationality. At first I felt hesitant and awkward as I met my six colleagues, all administrators like myself, in the offices of the Belgian CSD. Under the kindly guidance of the Belgian chairman my awkwardness soon began to disappear. The official languages of WEU were English and French, and there was an interpreter present. All the current members of the Committee spoke French, and this was the language most used not only during Committee meetings but in general chat in the corridor — hence the suggestion of my predecessor that it was very desirable that the British member should be able to speak French.

It was the custom of the Committee to meet in each of the seven member countries in turn. These meetings, which normally lasted two and a half days, were held not in the capital cities but in provincial towns, except in Belgium, where the chairman seemed to prefer his own office, and in Luxembourg, where Luxembourg city is the only town of any size. This was a very agreeable arrangement since it meant that over the next few years (and I remained British representative on the Committee for several years after I left the CSD) I found myself being paid to visit many interesting European towns and cities —

Montpellier, Avignon, Sarlat, Wiesbaden, Munich, Stuttgart, The Hague, Gouda, Amsterdam, Venice and Palermo, as well as Luxembourg and Brussels. When it was Britain's turn to be host, I arranged meetings in Edinburgh and Bath. My wife, fluent in French and German, came with me to all these meetings and we usually managed to combine them with a holiday.

Other aspects of the Committee's work were equally agreeable. The business did not involve conflicting interests or hard negotiations, and so discussions were relaxed and friendly — if slower at times than I would have wished. It was interesting to see how far in the attitudes of individual members, most of whom changed during my period of membership, the basic characteristics of the administrator were tempered by supposed national characteristics. While one or two of my colleagues tended to conform to the stereotypes cherished in Britain, most demonstrated a general urbanity more indicative of a particular class than a particular nation; and one Latin could almost have passed for the British stereotype of the Teuton.

Whoever was host usually contrived to arrange a rather more interesting meeting place than the universal type of office block. We met in the splendid early seventeenth century Town Hall in Gouda, in the medieval charter house in Villeneuve-les-Avignon, in the reconstructed Neues Schloss in Stuttgart, and in a palazzo on the Grand Canal in Venice. It was the custom at each meeting to have an excursion to a place of some government or administrative interest (though this was not interpreted too narrowly); and the hosts also arranged an official lunch or dinner. Some of these meals were memorable for the place or the food or both. The Luxembourg delegate, a *bon viveur* and gastronome, made up for the modest contribution he could make to discussions about the problems of large bureaucracies by offering us splendid examples of *haute cuisine* on the banks of the Moselle and in that part of his native land known as La Petite Suisse. In Venice we were taken one evening across the lagoon to the decaying splendour of the island of Torcello where, after viewing in the cathedral by way of aperitif the stunning Byzantine mosaics of the Last Judgement, we were entertained to dinner in the fashionable restaurant Cipriani.

The Italians were indeed most generous and imaginative hosts. The most memorable meeting — memorable for reasons not connected with the humdrum concerns of public administration — was held in Palermo. After travelling from Edinburgh in a succession of trains, stopping at interesting places on the way, and crossing the Straits of Messina on a train ferry, my wife and I arrived at the Sicilian capital one Sunday afternoon. The first impression of Sabbath calm was shattered when the taxi took us past the prison and we saw rioting prisoners scrambling about on the roof. Next day, having been well warned about the dangers to wallets and handbags, we saw something of a bustling noisy city where Phoenicians, Greeks, Romans, Arabs and Normans, not to mention French, Germans and Spaniards had at various periods in its long history held sway. On the Tuesday the Committee met in the headquarters of the Sicilian Council of Justice. In addition to addressing ourselves to our ordinary business as best we could in surroundings apparently designed as a stage set for grand opera, we were received in their offices in another part of the town by the President of the Sicilian Regional Government and the President of the Sicilian Assembly. The structure of government in Sicily was briefly explained to us. There was no mention of the Mafia, and we did not think it polite to raise the subject.

That evening the Regional Government were our hosts at an official dinner. We assembled as directed at 9 o'clock at the Grand Hotel Villa Igiea, formerly a stately home erected on the profits from the production of Marsala wine. We stood about awkwardly in a brooding nineteenth century salon waiting for the arrival of the President. In his absence no one offered any refreshments, and the local guests, none of whom at that stage seemed to speak any English or French, seemed even more awkward than we were. Well after 9.30 the President arrived, drinks were at last dispensed, and about 10 o'clock, weak and empty, we took our places at the table. Was that smoked salmon already set out on the plates? It was indeed; and not just any old smoked salmon; it was, according to the menu, *Salmone di Scozia affumicato*. What I now felt to be an oddly surrealist atmosphere was intensified when I learned that the Italian lady who was my neighbour at the table was a lecturer in Chinese. Fortunately she also spoke French, and soon proved to be an intelligent and agreeable companion.

The hospitality was not over. Next day there was lunch given by the Prefect, the senior local official of the Italian Government. Then we were taken in cars across the parched interior of Sicily to Agrigento to see the famous Doric temples erected in the fifth and sixth centuries BC. As we were leaving Agrigento, the sky clouded over, and we drove back in the dark through wind and driving rain. The storm raged all night. Next morning as we concluded our business, the wind howled, the rain drummed on the windows and palm trees were uprooted. We learned that the airport was closed and a ship had sunk — in the harbour. By the time my wife and I had to leave the shelter of the hotel to join the night sleeper train to Rome, the storm had abated. Miraculously, the taxi which we had ordered arrived on time, and we drove to the station at times up to the axles in flood water. We climbed aboard the train glad to think that we would be in Rome about 9 o'clock next morning.

Unusually, but the circumstances were unusual, we both took sleeping pills and were soon unconscious. We awoke as light was filtering in through the window screens. All was quiet. Where were we? Somewhere south of Rome no doubt. I pulled back the screen. We were standing at a station, and I saw the sign 'Enna'. Enna? . . . Enna was in Sicily! We were stuck about 3,000 feet above sea level in the centre of that stricken island. Part of the main line from Palermo along the north coast had been washed away, and we had been diverted on a secondary line across the mountains. For a while the silence remained unbroken. Eventually we moved off and reached the crossing to the mainland about the time we should have been arriving in Rome. After a very long, slow journey, stopping and starting all the way up the western coast of Italy, we reached Rome about 9.00 p.m.

We were tired, empty, but also curiously exhilarated. It had been a very interesting way to spend what had in fact been my last few days in the service of the Civil Service Department. Before leaving Edinburgh I had been told that after my Italian safari I would return to the Scottish Office on promotion to an under secretary post in the Scottish Education Department. I had enjoyed my four years with the CSD and the College, but was now very happy to be returning to St. Andrew's House to new and enlarged responsibilities. I was glad, however, that the CSD and the Scottish Office had agreed that I should continue for a time as British representative on the Public Administration Committee. The prospect of breaking out twice a year from what I feared might be the narrow world of Scottish education into wider European perspectives was very welcome — though I did not expect that any future meeting of the committee would be as memorable as these last few days in Palermo.

Chapter 10

Under Secretary — Education

Everyone has been at school, and nearly everyone has views of some kind on education. I was no exception. I was sceptical about what seemed to be the prevailing educational philosophy which tended to favour relaxed 'child-centred' methods of teaching. Was it right, I wondered, to be so critical of traditional teaching and the 3 R's? Were children properly prepared for all the realities of life outside the school if encouragement of their own creativity took precedence over teaching about the objective world and preparing them to cope with it? Was it wise to put children of all capabilities in the same class for some kind of egalitarian reasons rather than grouping them in accordance with their needs? Was it right that a publicly funded school system should be so organised as to promote religious apartheid? Was the widespread traditional admiration of Scottish education — which, curiously, seemed to co-exist with all kinds of criticism and dissent — anything more than another manifestation of the 'here's tae us; wha's like us?' syndrome?

Such scepticism was not in itself a reason for doubting whether I ought to be employed in a government education department. Civil servants are ordinary people with their share of ordinary diverse views on public issues. Their personal views are not obtruded in their work except to the extent that at senior level they have the opportunity to take part in the formation of policy, albeit not the major policies of the kind which form the content of party manifestos. After they have had their say, it is part of their professional discipline at all levels to promote and implement as well as they can policies with which they may be out of sympathy.

SED had the reputation in some parts of St. Andrew's House of being a rather old-fashioned department. Certainly, it had a longer pedigree than some

129

of the recent upstarts, having started life in the mid-nineteenth century as the Scotch Education Department. For long it had been run by professional educators. It was only just before the second World War that administrative grade civil servants had been appointed to its senior staff; and it was many years after the war before it conformed to ordinary Civil Service practice by having an administrator as Secretary. The professional staff were not merely educational advisers; they were Her Majesty's Inspectors of Schools. The names of the Inspectors in the basic grade were preceded in any formal context by the letters HMI (e.g. HMI Mr Brown); those of more senior Inspectors followed more elaborate collections of capital letters.

Responsibility for the educational work of the SED — the Department was, curiously, also responsible for Social Work Services — was divided among three under secretaries. Martin Fearn, hitherto the occupant of one of these under secretary posts, had been promoted to Secretary of the Department on the retiral of Sir Norman Graham and I was to fill his place. I inherited his room, and, more important, a first-class senior personal secretary, Iris Paterson, who had served him well and who was to serve me well for the next ten years. My neighbour in the next room was HMSCI Mr James McGarrity, who as Senior Chief Inspector was head of the Inspectorate.

One of my under secretary colleagues dealt with the schools, their organisation and administration, and what went on inside them; the other covered further education and the arts; and I dealt mainly with resources, that is, staff and buildings. My private views on the content of education were unlikely to have much direct relevance to my new official responsibilities. I had three divisions, each under an assistant secretary; one was concerned with educational buildings of all kinds, the second looked after the supply and training of teachers, and the third dealt with the salaries and conditions of service of teachers, along with the management of Colleges of Education.

The first of these divisions, though important in itself, did not take up much of my time. Ian Hamilton, the assistant secretary, was well used to dealing with local authorities when they sought approval from the Department to start new building — and was accustomed too to sit at the minister's right hand when they tried to persuade him that the Department was being too restrictive or ungenerous. There were other more general issues on his side in which I was involved. We had, for example, to settle in consultation with ministers and Treasury the total annual sums available for educational building. We tried to reduce, and did in time reduce, the number of stages at which departmental approval of building schemes was required. Schools were, after all, fairly simple structures with few of the complex design problems and elaborate engineering services of a large general hospital; and part of the reason for local government reorganisation which came along in 1975 was that authorities should be large enough and responsible enough to manage with less oversight from central government.

On the teachers front I was much more heavily involved. Shortly before my arrival the Department had published a report on the number of teachers required in secondary schools. This was the result of a study by James McGarrity and colleagues, both administrative and professional, of the current staffing in schools and what would be a realistic if not ideal pattern for the future, taking account not only of school size but the mix of subjects taught. It soon became known as the 'Red Book' — a reference to the colour of the cover, not to any revolutionary doctrine contained within. It was consulted, referred to and argued over in the Department, in the offices of education authorities and in the schools, as much as any classic scholarly text. For the first time there was available an authoritative set of staffing standards which could determine the need for teachers not only for individual schools but also for different authorities and for Scotland as a whole. It was generally if cautiously welcomed as a useful guide, if not an arbiter for every situation.

The staffing of the schools and teacher numbers were questions on which ministers were closely interested. I was soon busy with my colleagues in the preparation of notes and 'submissions' (as the more important memoranda going to the ministers were called), and in meetings in ministerial offices on the fifth floor. During my first few weeks in SED the Heath government was in office. Gordon Campbell was Secretary of State for Scotland and Hector Monro was Parliamentary Under Secretary of State responsible for education. But the miners' strike and the 3-day week precipitated a general election early in 1974, and Labour returned to power. Willie Ross, the principal scourge of erstwhile Scottish ministers, became Secretary of State and Robert Hughes, Parliamentary Under Secretary.

While the Red Book was the basis of calculations of teacher requirements in the medium and long term, there was an immediate short-term problem about which ministers were understandably very exercised. The school leaving age had recently been raised from 15 to 16. Some authorities, those in the north-east for example, had more than an adequate supply of teachers to meet the new demands on the schools; but others, particularly in parts of the west of Scotland which had a history of staffing problems, found great difficulty in trying to ensure that every class always had a teacher. In fact many schools had to admit defeat, and some pupils were sent home for part of the day. Pupils might or might not have resented 'part-time education', but it was certainly a hot potato for politicians. Local authorities, not government ministers, were responsible for running the schools and staffing them; but no one paid much attention to such constitutional niceties. Education was one of the responsibilities of the Secretary of State for Scotland, and he controlled the number of teachers being trained in the Colleges. If education was not provided because there were not enough teachers, it was his fault. Parliamentary Questions flowed in thick and fast, and even though new ministers could at that stage blame their predecessors, they were not greatly pleased.

If this was the short-term problem, the long-term problem, as sometimes happens, was completely the reverse. As well as preparing reports about shortages and doing what we could to reduce them, we had to tell ministers that before very long, unless some correcting action was taken, there would be too many teachers. The birth rate had increased steadily in the fifties and early sixties, but after 1964, the peak year, it had been falling year by year. This was already reducing the number of pupils in the primary schools and would soon begin to affect numbers in the secondary schools. Over the next decade the school population would drop substantially, and, even allowing for improved staffing standards, we would need fewer teachers. For the immediate present no precipitate action need be taken, but soon we would need to consider reducing the intake to Colleges of Education — and perhaps the number of Colleges.

I did not foresee then that the question of College closures was to involve me in the major drama of my career in SED. Meanwhile another drama was about to begin.

Teachers were as much concerned as everyone else about their salary levels as inflation seemed to bound ahead. Salary negotiations were conducted by the Scottish Teachers' Salaries Committee (STSC). The employers' side consisted mainly of representatives of the education authorities, but there were also two representatives of the Secretary of State; on the teachers' side were representatives of the professional associations. I succeeded Martin Fearn as the senior representative of the Secretary of State; George Fair, one of my assistant secretaries, was the other. We looked forward to a lively time during the next round of salary negotiations, since teachers had recently become more convinced than ever that they had fallen well behind in the salary race.

But events took a different course. Soon after they came to office the Labour Government decided to appoint a committee under the chairmanship of Lord Houghton, a Labour peer, to carry out a fundamental review of teachers' pay both in England and Wales and in Scotland, and to make recommendations for the future. Was this the result of a genuine belief that only a special review could do justice in what was a thoroughly unsatisfactory situation? Or did it flow from a desire to placate a group which, according to current folklore, contained a high proportion of Labour supporters? Perhaps a little of both — though I never knew. In any event, it was not an unreasonable decision. Other groups, doctors and dentists for example, had in their time had special reviews of pay and no doubt others would follow — though such by-passing the normal negotiating machinery without compelling reason could create trouble. If everyone is a special case, no one is a special case. Instead of preparing for battle in the STSC, George Fair and I began preparing a memorandum of evidence for Lord Houghton and his committee.

Such documents go through several drafts and are the basis of much consultation before they see the light of day. The general scene had to be set and recent history recounted. While we did not think it right to make specific recommendations about what increases should be given, we had to set out the Department's views on the factors, including for example supply and distribution, which had a bearing on the pay of different types of teachers, with different qualifications in different kinds of educational establishments. Inspectors and other colleagues made their contributions; differences of view had to be resolved; the Secretary, a veteran of many negotiations on teachers' pay, went over our draft with that attention to detail for which he was well known; and finally ministers had to approve it. All the time we had to keep in touch with the Department of Education and Science. Although we were dealing with different groups of teachers, on different current salaries, both Departments had to ensure that no one would be able to play one off against the other.

The various teachers' organisations also made their submissions to Houghton. They were not so diffident about making detailed recommendations on figures, and they argued for increases of the order of 30%–35%.

After reading the mass of evidence presented to them the committee arranged to take oral evidence. One day I led a departmental team into their committee room. Lord Houghton and his colleagues subjected us to a thorough if civilised grilling. But we survived; and in our post-mortem outside we agreed that while they might not accept all we said, they had not managed to uncover any serious gaps in knowledge or defects in argument.

While these exchanges between Houghton and the interested parties were going on, relations between the teachers and the Government in Scotland had

133

become very strained. The Scottish teachers argued that since Houghton would recommend major increases in pay — inflation alone justified significant improvement — an interim increase should be awarded while the committee were at work. In comparable situations in other fields interim increases were not unknown; but, curiously, teachers in England and Wales, apparently more philosophic than their Scottish colleagues, made no comparable demand. The Scottish teaching unions prepared to make a formal claim to the STSC.

Ministers decided that the claim should be resisted. It was not known what Houghton would recommend, and an interim increase might lead to over-payment and subsequent anguish when money had to be recovered. Moreover, any increase now in Scotland, however modest, would almost certainly disturb the calm reigning in England. Apart from all that, no interim increase would make teachers any better off at the end of the day, and Houghton was likely to report within months.

George and I, as the Secretary of State's representatives on the employers' side, were instructed to take this line. We knew that the representatives of the education authorities, who greatly outnumbered us, were sympathetic to the teachers' claim, and we doubted whether on this occasion our power of argument and persuasion, not to mention the good relations which we had with them, would be sufficient to make them line up with the Government. Was this a case, we wondered, for playing a special card which normally remained tucked away in our brief-cases?

When the STSC had been established, a 'concordat' had been drawn up between the Secretary of State and the education authorities by which before any offer could be made by the employers' side the Secretary of State's representatives had to agree to the total sum involved if not all the details. He after all had to meet the greater part of the cost of any increases. This power to veto a proposed offer had never in fact been used. We were now instructed to use it if our exposition of the Government's arguments failed to win the day.

At the meeting of the employers' side George and I did our best, but in spite of all our efforts, our colleagues were not to be convinced. I had to play the final card. I referred to the concordat. The Secretary of State, I said, was not prepared to agree to any interim increase, and therefore the employers' side was not authorised to offer one. There was a momentary silence; and then there spread over the faces round the table expressions of astonishment, pain and disgust. The message of the ensuing hubbub was clear. The authorities' representatives did not agree with the Secretary of State's attitude to the claim, but, more important, they resented and were affronted by the first-ever use of the veto. It was all the more awkward for them as the teachers would have to be told that it was the employers' side not the Secretary of State that rejected their claim. Our good relations with the councillors and officials who were the authorities' representatives had suddenly gone sour, and it was a very chilly and discomfited employers' side that met the teachers a short while later.

The spokesman for the employers said that while they were very sympathetic to the teachers' position they could not accept the claim. The reasons he gave were those which a short while before I had been expounding to him and his now stony-faced colleagues. There was no suggestion that unexpected cards had been played or reluctant arms twisted. The reaction of the teachers surprised no one. In addition to the routine expression of shock and astonishment there was a good deal of colourful rhetoric about the mood of the profession and threats that the representatives present might not be able to prevent some form of direct action.

Various forms of direct action did indeed follow. There were demonstrations in the streets, and here and there pupils had time off because teachers were on strike. No one seemed to have any doubt who was responsible for keeping the teachers in poverty; and ex-teacher Willie Ross found himself assailed in the press, in Parliament and in the streets as the enemy of the profession. I was in and out of his office a great deal during this period. Returning to my own office after one of these sessions I slightly startled the unflappable Iris Paterson by asking her to take down for the first time in her career, and in mine, the draft of a minute for the Secretary of State to send urgently to the Prime Minister.

The Government remained unmoved by all the pressure, and in December the Houghton Committee produced its report. The general effect was to recommend increases of rather more than 25% for teachers in schools, and slightly more for those in further education, to be paid retrospectively from May. Not all the details were filled in, and it was left to the negotiating body to devise a new structure of pay in the light of the recommendations. The employers' side met early in the New Year. George Fair and I had with us Gordon Brewerton, one of George's principals, who was the expert on increments, allowances, assimilation and the other esoteric but necessary details of the teachers' salary structures. Hard feelings were forgotten, and with the authorities' representatives we considered what might be the details and small print of an agreement with the teachers. That agreement was reached very quickly, and relations between the two sides, nourished by very substantial increases for the teachers, returned to their normal state of wary respect.

It was only a few months before the normal annual round of pay negotiations began in the spring. By then a major reorganisation of local government in Scotland had taken place. Counties, cities and burghs were no more: regions and districts had taken their place. The result was a smaller number of on average larger and, it was hoped, more efficient authorities. The 12 regions, which were the education authorities, provided the representatives for the newly-constituted employers' side of the STSC. The former chairman, a couthie character from East Lothian ('ma wee coontie') was succeeded by George Foulkes, Lothian Region councillor and former student politician, whose eyes were fixed on the road to Westminster.

Pay policy was now one of the Government's major concerns. Inflation was running high in the mid-seventies — at one stage the annual rate was over 25% — and exercising some kind of control over pay increases was thought to be a necessary contribution to controlling it. No one on either side of the STSC supposed that teachers generally, having had a major increase following Houghton, could expect more than the going rate during the next annual rounds. But what was the going rate? The generalities of government policies, which themselves changed from time to time, had to be translated into more specific statements which I could make to the employers' representatives. I had to know how far I could go without the wrath of the Treasury, the Department of Employment and the Department of Education and Science, not to mention the Secretary of State, falling upon my head. Alas, George Fair, my ever-resourceful companion in arms, had suffered a severe heart attack — he was later to die as the result of another — and was no longer with me; and Roger Smith, his successor, was new to all this rough and tumble.

I did not find it surprising during this period that the Government did all they could to gain the support of the Trades Unions for their policies; but I did find it extraordinary at one stage that they merely adopted the TUC's policies as their own. One White Paper was published which, after making the usual points about the need to limit pay increases, said that the Government would follow the policy recommended in a TUC paper which was reproduced in an appendix. This seemed to be a surrender by the Government to one group of powerful vested interests. I had always remembered one lesson from the history books — the danger to good government when 'overmighty subjects' had too much power. This kow-towing to the unions would, I thought, lead to trouble not only for the community at large but for the Government themselves. (And in due course it did. In a few years when the Callaghan Government sought to take a tough line on pay — too tough, for by that stage a 5% maximum increase was unrealistic — the unions thought they could put them in their place. The disruption of the 'winter of discontent' led to an election and the return of a Tory Government.)

I became inured to the gruff and sometimes surly manner in which Willie Ross conducted official business. Happily, I never experienced one of the ferocious attacks which could follow a comment or suggestion which displeased him. These onslaughts could descend on friends or foes alike. Once when summoned to see him I had to wait in his outer office while an interview with a senior political supporter ran beyond its expected time. The private secretary became restive and decided to take some papers into the inner sanctum. When he came out I asked him what was happening. The short reply told it all: 'He's kicking him all round the park.'

Willie Ross had many sterling qualities, but I was never impressed by his capacity to handle figures. In all these arguments about pay, anyone who could skilfully toss figures to and fro, acknowledging a point here but responding with another telling point there, had a real advantage. The Secretary of State never took part personally in negotiations, but more than once he had to appear on TV or on radio to justify Government policy. He was never at his best in such encounters, and a rather wooden doggedness, spiced now and again with ritual denunciations of Tories and other bogey-men, did not entirely make up for a lack of nimbleness with statistics. On the other hand his political antennae were always in good working order. Once when we hurtled through Glasgow led by a police car with siren blaring in order to reach the TV studios on time, he slumped down in the back seat of the car so that his face could not be seen from the outside. 'This is the quickest way to lose votes,' he growled at me.

If as a result of these annual battles about salaries the teachers' representatives managed to gain no more than something like the going rate, they were determined to improve their lot on another front. A separate negotiating committee constituted on the same lines as the STSC dealt with conditions of service. After some years with not much happening, it sprang to life when the teachers decided to press for a 'teachers' contract'. Most if not all teachers already had contracts of some kind with their employers, but their representatives now wanted these contracts to include some provision about maximum sizes of classes, and hours of work. With the statisticians, we had to do some intensive homework to work out the consequences which such ambitions would have for the staffing of schools. Happily, we were able to reach a settlement which did not overall produce a demand for teachers greater than was implied by the staffing standards in the Red Book. And so, with less anguish than I had feared, the teachers got their contracts, and maximum class sizes were for the first time fixed.

Negotiations or preparing for negotiations occupied much of my time during these years, but between, and indeed during, these periods of sometimes hectic activity, the ordinary work of the Department went on — correspondence, PQs, minutes, and, of course, meetings.

There were two important kinds of departmental meeting which the Secretary chaired. First, there was the Departmental Planning Committee, consisting of under secretaries, the Senior Chief Inspector and a few others, which looked at the major developments in education and their implications for the future. Second, there were meetings, largely as it happened of the same individuals, to consider allocations of finance for capital investment — what should be included in our bids to the Treasury and, when we had our total departmental allocation, how it should be distributed. These discussions and their conclusions — all subject of course, to the approval of the Secretary of State — concerned not only schools and colleges of all kinds: they also included provision for the Arts and Museums. One project in that field had been around for some time — the construction of a building somewhere in the Glasgow area to house the art collection which Sir William Burrell had left to the city. I remember in my earlier days it was regularly squeezed out; but I remember too the occasion on which it was finally squeezed in.

All the important bodies in the educational world wanted to make their views known to the Department and influence Government policy, and the Department was no less interested to meet them since it was these bodies which implemented Government policy on the ground. We had meetings with the Educational Committee of COSLA (the Convention of Scottish Local Authorities) chaired by the ubiquitous George Foulkes, and with representatives of the Directors of Education. The latter group tended naturally to be closer to the realities near the chalk face than the former. More frequent meetings took place with the Principals of the Colleges of Education. The Department did not run the schools; but, since it met the costs of the Colleges, it sometimes came close to running the Colleges. These encounters were usually lively, but the liveliness could take a tiresome turn as there were prima donnas of both sexes among the Principals.

Most of these meetings with outside bodies now took place not in St. Andrew's House, but in a cheap (at least it looked cheap) and nasty new building nearby. St. Andrew's House had never been able to accommodate all the staff of the Secretary of State's departments, many of whom had been

138

scattered about in assorted premises all over Edinburgh. A large new office had been planned as part of a commercial development near the east end of Princes Street. Along with St. Andrew's House this would provide accommodation for most of the Secretary of State's staff. Not only that, it was to be the new headquarters of the Scottish Office in which ministers and most of the senior staff would have their offices. This new building, known as New St. Andrew's House, was formally opened by the Queen in July 1975, and included among its occupants the Secretary of the SED, my two under secretary colleagues and all their staff.

Presumably no one had actually intended that it should be one of the ugliest buildings in Edinburgh, but that is what it was (and is). I was more than happy to stay with my staff in what was now known as Old St. Andrew's House. The conference rooms of the new building had for some curious reason no windows, and I was always glad at the end of the meetings with the COSLA Education Committee and other educational bodies to get out into the daylight and fresh air and wend my way back to my slightly old fashioned room in 'Old' St. Andrew's House.

In that far from old building, now deserted by ministers and the very top brass, my colleagues and I were drawing up proposals for the amalgamation and closure of Colleges of Education — proposals which we knew would lead to the biggest rumpus in Scottish education for many years. Ministers had agreed in the light of our indications of the consequences of the reduced birth-rate and the need to train fewer teachers that there was at least an arguable case for reducing the number of Colleges of Education. We had been commissioned to draw up for their consideration a draft paper which would set out the whole problem and indicate the action which might be taken. When its terms were finally agreed it would be the basis for consultation with all the interested parties before any final decisions were made.

During the latter part of 1976 there were many meetings round my table of those involved in preparing the paper. The key people were the assistant secretaries in charge of the two divisions concerned — Kenneth Forbes and Roger Smith — and Joan Sandison, the Chief Inspector responsible for teacher training. Kenneth Forbes, who dealt with the supply of teachers, had himself started his professional life as a teacher and had been a Chief Inspector in the Department before transferring to the administrative side. (Having proved himself as a first class administrator he was later to be appointed Director of the Scottish Prison Service, and did an excellent job in that difficult post before he tragically died suddenly as the result of a heart attack.) Roger's responsibility

139

was the administration of the Colleges of Education. Unlike his predecessor, George Fair, who had joined the Civil Service in the basic clerical grade and then steadily climbed the hierarchy, he was a member of a once fairly numerous but now far from common species in the higher ranks of the Service — a classics man from Cambridge. Joan Sandison's wide experience and authority on matters educational went far beyond the field of domestic science in which she had been a teacher and a teacher of teachers before entering the Inspectorate. We had with us from time to time principals from the two divisions, and, very important, representatives of the Statistics Branch.

Statistics were indeed the origin of the whole exercise. Critics of the paper — and we expected that most of those consulted would be highly critical of the heretical proposition that Scotland needed fewer teachers and fewer Colleges of Education — would inevitably attack its statistical base. They would seek to show that the figures were wrong or at least unsoundly based, and not a sure foundation for radical change. And so we cast very critical eyes over birth-rates, projected school populations and expected numbers of teachers.

No one, not even those most likely to attack departmental figures, could deny that over the last ten years birth-rates had been falling dramatically. In 1964, over 104,000 children had been born in Scotland; in 1975, there were fewer than 68,000. The consequences for school rolls could be easily worked out. The effect of other factors influencing the size of rolls and the future need for teachers was not so easily determined. No one could be sure when the steady fall in the birth-rate would come to an end — whether, in fact it might not begin to rise in the following year. Moreover, assumptions had to be made — and they could only be assumptions — about future 'wastage' from the teaching profession and the ranks of students in training. But allowing for these and other uncertainties and for a margin of error in all the calculations, there was no doubt that for many years ahead school rolls would fall and fewer teachers would need to be trained to meet the staffing standards of the Red Book. There was no justification for continuing to spend public money on running ten Colleges of Education which had been designed in the days of steadily rising birth-rates to train far more teachers than the numbers now required. We debated which Colleges might be closed or amalgamated, bearing in mind geography, existing facilities and other relevant factors. We considered what arrangements might be made for College staff made redundant. We knew that even if after public argument and debate it was agreed that some closure or amalgamation was justified, there would be spirited opposition from those directly affected to whatever particular proposals were put forward.

Kenneth coordinated the drafting of the paper and the re-drafting which followed our meetings. When I was content with its form and content, it went forward to the Secretary; and when he was content it was submitted to the Secretary of State (now Bruce Millan) through the Parliamentary Under Secretary responsible for education (Frank McElhone). There was further to-ing and fro-ing with ministers. The paper which was published in January 1977 following these exchanges proposed reductions in the number of students admitted for teacher training, the closure of one College (Craigie College, Ayr) and two amalgamations involving another four. The number of Colleges would be reduced to seven.

As expected, the paper produced an outburst of criticism, not to say anger and denunciation, in the press, in Parliament and in the educational world. The dial-a-quote brigade were quick to give immediate comments (Teddy Taylor MP professed to be 'horrified'); and soon the PQs and requests for meetings were flowing in. It was only to be expected that people who had devoted much of their professional lives to running educational establishments whose future was under threat and whose own jobs were possibly to disappear should be concerned about the proposals in the paper, however adequate the arrangements for redundancy. We were soon involved in a series of meetings at which representatives of educational bodies of all kinds commented on and argued against the proposals, sometimes angrily, occasionally constructively.

For the next three months I and members of my little group found our official lives dominated and our private lives disrupted by the spectres of redundant Colleges. At some of these meetings I was in the chair accompanied by my colleagues. We tried to bring home to those on the other side of the table the implications of current demographic trends. Some of them accepted the trends but disputed our assessment of the implications; others seemed to think that expansion was the natural order of things in education, or if expansion could not go on indefinitely, the status quo certainly could. Comments on the paper were occasionally accompanied by comments on its anonymous authors — their limited understanding, or their suspect motives. None were more outspoken in that vein than the representatives of the Association of Lecturers in Colleges of Education in Scotland (ALCES) led by Mr John Maxton, later to become MP for Cathcart.

On other occasions one or other minister was in the chair. While civil servants have inhibitions about responding too forcefully to intemperate attacks — they are after all only the servants of the ministers and must do nothing to make life more difficult for them — ministers themselves, if so

141

disposed, need feel no such restraints. ALCES, dissatisfied with their meeting with me and my colleagues, demanded to see Bruce Millan, and he agreed to meet them. As an accountant he was well used to handling figures, and was master of the case presented in the paper. Though regarded by some as a grey man, he could be forceful and tenacious. Concerned as he was about lecturers' jobs, he was not to be deflected from the logic of the arguments in the paper. When Maxton and his colleagues attacked the paper, its figures and its recommendations, he not only rebutted their arguments; as one of my colleagues put it afterwards, he quietly wiped the floor with them.

Frank McElhone was not so ready to counter-attack when he was in the chair at one of these meetings. The whole argument turned on statistics, and numeracy was not the most obvious of his many qualities. On one occasion at least, there may have been other reasons for his reluctance to weigh in. A meeting was arranged at which he would hear the views of the Roman Catholic bishops. They were particularly concerned about a proposal that Craiglockhart College in Edinburgh, a College for training Catholic teachers, should be merged with Moray House, a non-denominational college in the same city, a proposal which included various safeguards to preserve the religious basis of the training of Catholic students. Joan Sandison and I accompanied him. The minister, who was himself a Catholic, surprised us by saying at the outset that while he was, of course, associated with the proposals in the paper, the people who knew most about them were sitting by his side, and he would ask them to deal with comments and questions. We were then attacked by an exceedingly testy Archbishop who, after complaining about the inadequate number of copies of the paper and the address to which they had been sent, then largely ignored its arguments and accused us of mounting an attack on Catholic education. Joan and I responded with Christian forbearance and official circumspection. None of the other bishops showed the same combative spirit as their principal spokesman, but the discussion ended with no meeting of minds. Later, when we ourselves met Craiglockhart College and other Catholic representatives, they made their points fairly in a much more irenic atmosphere.

We also had meetings with representatives of the press and went over the figures with them. The proposed closure of Colleges was a good story for the more up-market journals; it was highly controversial and even these journals like controversy as much as news. The *Scotsman* seldom thought well of anything emerging from St. Andrew's House, and their education correspondent saw no reason for making an exception in relation to College closures. The Scottish edition of the *Times Educational Supplement* also weighed in against the proposals. The Government were clearly having no more success with the press than with the educational establishment.

But it was in Parliament that the crucial and most dramatic encounters took place. MPs of all parties were incensed by the Government's proposals. They put down dozens of Questions to the Secretary of State and were not impressed by the Answers they received. A debate in the Scottish Grand Committee was arranged for one morning in February. My colleagues and I prepared the usual draft opening speech for the Secretary of State, collected masses of background briefing material, transported ourselves to London and presented ourselves in the Secretary of State's room in Dover House on the morning of the day before the debate. We had another talk with him in the afternoon after which we retired to the attics to recast some of the material. Eventually we escaped from Dover House late in the evening, our duty, for that day, we hoped, well and truly done.

Next morning, before the debate started, word came that the Secretary of State had decided in the light of the widespread discontent among Members of all parties that he should offer a second morning's debate two days later on Thursday. Officially that posed us no problem. The personal problems — beds for two extra nights, clean shirts for two extra days, and domestic complications in Edinburgh — were put to the back of our minds as we sorted out papers and watched MPs taking their places.

Bruce Millan opened the debate with an exposition of the problem and the action he proposed to take to deal with it. There followed a succession of speeches denouncing the paper, its arguments and its conclusions. Teddy Taylor, spluttering with righteous indignation, led the predictable attacks for the Tory benches; but the Government supporters on the Labour benches were no less eager to tell the Secretary of State how wrong he was and what little support he could expect from them. In the closing minutes, Bruce Millan wound up the debate as effectively, so it seemed to us, as he had opened it — and, it also seemed, to equally little effect.

During the next forty-eight hours our principal task was to brief and prepare a draft speech for Frank McElhone who on Thursday was to face the attacking Tories, with behind him a mass of disaffected Government supporters. Was there anything new to say?

New or not, something relevant and, we hoped, persuasive, at least to minds open to argument, was put together for the minister to use. We met him in his room in the House on the Wednesday afternoon. With no commitments for the evening, and aware that he was a prisoner in the Palace of Westminster until the last vote about 10.00 p.m., he was in a very relaxed and chatty mood, full of what Glaswegians like to regard as typical Glasgow bonhomie. After indicating that the speech was fine, he was clearly disposed to move on to other subjects. He conducted us on an exhilarating tour not only of the current political horizon, but of the basic motives, methods and mores of politicians. Particularly fascinating was his analysis of the relationship between the Roman Catholic Church and the Labour Party, the attitude of that Church to some of his non-Catholic colleagues, and the implications of the pill for Catholic women. By the time we left his room we too were relaxed and stimulated and ready for further convivial chat among ourselves over a good meal. (Whatever the crisis of the Colleges did or did not do for us, it enlarged our gastronomic experience. Evenings in London were spent in a variety of restaurants; and many years later we still remembered convivial gatherings in Bertorelli's, Simpson's in the Strand, Chez Solange and the White Tower. We liked to take the smooth with the rough.)

We came down to earth next morning. The resumed debate in the Scottish Grand Committee was a re-run of Tuesday's performance at a lower intellectual level and in an even testier atmosphere. From time to time I gained a certain uplift by looking out of the windows across the Thames to St. Thomas' Hospital and the world outside where ordinary people were going about their business. Towards the end of the debate the shouting and the barracking increased as, to the astonishment of the Labour benches, some English Tory MPs drifted into the room and took their seats on the benches opposite. These were the Tory members for English constituencies who had been appointed to the Scottish Grand Committee in order that its party balance should be the same as that of the whole House (where the Labour majority was not as great as among the Scottish MPs). They had never appeared — until today. Soon the nature of the ploy became clear, and the debate dissolved in uproar. When the vote was taken at 1.00 p.m. the serried ranks of Tories plus the many Labour members determined not to follow their leader managed between them to inflict a heavy defeat on the Government. Amid the shouting and general disorder, we crept out into the corridor. It was not necessary for the Government to have Parliamentary approval for changes in the recruitment of student teachers or the organisation of the Colleges, and so the loss of the vote did not in itself mean that the whole plan was scuppered. But there was no doubt that the morning's vote was a blow to the Government.

Ministers did not take long to decide that they should shrug off what they regarded as a temporary set-back. There was no reason to abandon the overwhelming logic of the policy set out in the paper. The Secretary of State went on to defend the policy on television. There were further meetings in Edinburgh with representatives of the Colleges. The PQs continued to flood in and the Answers showed no wavering. In-trays on the desks of Kenneth Forbes and Roger Smith were bright with green folders and their staffs were very busy preparing draft replies. One evening Frank McElhone filibustered in splendid style for over twenty-five minutes in an Adjournment Debate after Tam Dalyell had put his Honourable Friend on the spot by taking not much more than two minutes of the available half hour merely to say he wanted replies to questions he had raised during the earlier debate in the Scottish Grand Committee.

The official Opposition succeeded in arranging a half-day debate on the floor of the House itself. That a little local difficulty in Scottish education, not regarded as the most exciting subject at Westminster, should engage the attention of the whole House showed the power and determination of the opposition to the Secretary of State's proposals both in and out of Parliament. I wrote yet another draft speech on what was by now a very well worn subject. There were the usual briefings with the Secretary of State and Frank McElhone, changes here and re-casting there, and last minute calls for the typists. The debate was surprisingly constructive and orderly until in his winding-up Frank McElhone began to bait the Opposition rather than deal with their arguments. In the Division the Government were once again defeated.

This defeat was much more serious. In spite of a two-line whip many Labour members had voted with the Tories or abstained, after a full-dress debate in the House itself. The Secretary of State, though quite unconvinced by the arguments against him, decided to think again about how best, granted all the opposition, to carry forward some reorganisation of the College system.

I did not participate for long on this reconsideration. Very soon I was transferred to an under secretary vacancy which had emerged on the health service side of SHHD. It was with some regret I left my colleagues in SED and the unfinished business of the Colleges. The Labour Government never in fact managed to carry out any significant reorganisation of the College system. It was only when the Conservatives returned to power in 1979 that the logic against which they had battled so vigorously if not sensibly in opposition became evident to them. The need for closures and amalgamation as argued in their predecessors' first consultation paper was accepted. Closure and amalgamation took place, if not exactly as envisaged in that paper. Mr George Younger, MP for Ayr, was now Secretary of State for Scotland and Craigie College for one remained open. But long before then I was immersed in other things.

Chapter 11

Under Secretary — Health Services

In the summer of 1977 when I was moved back to the Scottish Home and Health Department I felt as if I was returning home. However much I might regret leaving SED while the question of the redundant Colleges was unresolved, and, more particularly, leaving colleagues who had soldiered with me through some lively campaigns, I looked forward to working once more in the field in which I had spent most of my official career. I knew my way around the health service, and had no personal doubts or reservations as I had in education about the objects of the exercise. The aim of the health service, simply put, was to promote health, and cure or alleviate sickness. Ideas about social engineering did not complicate the issue.

There were two under secretary posts on the health service side of SHHD. One dealing with resources — staff, buildings, supplies — was analogous in some respects to the post I was leaving in SED. It was occupied by John Walker with whom I had worked happily in the past. I was glad I was to occupy the other, which was concerned with the whole range of services to patients and the organisation of the service as a whole. I installed myself in Room 117 on the first floor of St. Andrew's House. Here from the earliest days of the National Health Service, there had sat a succession of under secretaries, forbidding senior figures as they had seemed to me when I was young.

Although I was moving home, I did not expect the old homestead to look exactly as I had left it in 1969. At that time I had been busy with consultation about reorganisation of the so-called 'tripartite service' in which there had been different local bodies responsible for hospitals, general practitioner services and public health. A major reorganisation had subsequently been carried through, and since 1974 fifteen health boards had been responsible for all aspects of the service in their areas. That was certainly a change for the better. I was not so happy about the new structure of advisory and consultative bodies which had been set up at national and local levels. It was of course essential to have as good advice as could be got on specialist or technical questions (e.g. when should children be vaccinated or inoculated; against what?). It was also necessary to have some consultation within the service about more general issues. But 'participation' had been one of the fashionable concepts of the early seventies, and it seemed to me that that apparatus of consultation now written in to the statute was too complex and unwieldy — a view which I soon learned many, but by no means all, of those involved seemed to share.

The 1974 reorganisation had been carried through by a Conservative Government, but the Labour Government now in power showed no disposition to make structural changes. In fact, there was a broad if unacknowledged consensus between the parties on the main structure of the NHS. On one peripheral issue — the provision of private beds in hospitals — there was certainly sharp disagreement; and the Conservatives claimed they would run the service more efficiently and get better value for money. But it did not seem likely that there would be major policy changes for some time whatever Government was in power. Assuming my new post was to be my last before retiral in 1983 at age 60 (the general rule for administrative staff in the Scottish Office) it seemed as if I would be concerned with efforts to improve and expand the service rather than to make any fundamental changes.

The election of 1979 brought in a Conservative Government, but that first Thatcher administration, unlike its successors, did not take any new radical approach to the provision of health services. Our day-to-day activities and concerns were largely unchanged. The senior civil servant's lot is of course affected by the ministers under whom he works — their personalities, styles of work, intellectual ability, sensitivity to people and problems, and the firmness or otherwise with which they pursue their aims. Some ministers may be hard taskmasters, but easy-going ministers are not necessarily easy to work with — minds may take too long to be made up, or are too easily changed. Without attempting what might be thought an impertinent analysis of the performances of individuals still active in public life, let me merely say that working with Bruce Millan (Labour) on the one hand and his Conservative successor as Secretary of State George Younger (now Lord Younger) on the other was not so different as comparison of the rather cool and remote manner of the first with the easy charm of the second might suggest. I had many more dealings with the Parliamentary Under Secretaries. If there were differences between the style and performance of Labour's Harry Ewing (now Lord Ewing) and his Conservative successor Russell (now Sir Russell) Fairgrieve, both were genial characters with whom it was easy to form good working relationships.

And so, even though Russell Fairgrieve was succeeded in turn by Allan Stewart and John (now Lord) Mackay, during the whole of my six years in Room 117 I worked along the same lines, seeking broadly the same goals, dealing most of the time with the same kind of problems. I had 'reporting' to me (as the Civil Service has it) four assistant secretaries and their staffs, and a Principal Medical Officer who was in charge of the Planning Unit established as part of the 1974 reorganisation. I in turn reported to the Secretary of the Department, Archie Rennie, though much of the time I dealt direct with the Parliamentary Under Secretary. On any question which looked as if it would involve the Secretary of State personally there was seldom any doubt that it had to go through the Secretary. It might be different when dealing with successive chapters of a long saga; and such sagas were always with us. (One, concerning a proposal by the Ayrshire and Arran health board to close a rather run-down hospital in George Younger's constituency, lasted over a year.)

The National Health Service in Scotland employed at the end of the 1970s about 120,000 people, and it spent annually over £700 million of taxpayers' money. Almost the whole population were on the lists of general practitioners; about three quarters of a million patients occupied acute hospital beds during the year; and there were annually nearly two million new out-patients. For the provision of all this care and treatment the Secretary of State was responsible to Parliament. Even if he were assisted in his office by the brightest of administrative talents, he could not effectively run an organisation of this size from his own office. Hence the importance of the fifteen health boards. They did not take over the Secretary of State's responsibilities; they ran the service on his behalf within the broad policies he laid down and the finances he made available. This meant that there had to be a close relationship between the Secretary of State and his office on the one hand and the boards on the other. The Secretary of State appointed the members of the boards, and the running of the NHS was in effect a partnership in which there was continual contact taking many forms between the boards and the Secretary of State's office, i.e. the Department.

Regular meetings between the Department and officials of the boards provided one of the most important types of contact — one series for Chairmen, and others for Chief Administrative Medical Officers, Secretaries, Treasurers and other specialists. At these meetings we discussed what was happening on the ground, and considered possible changes in policies and priorities. Officials of the boards were never slow to make the day-to-day problems of the service, as they saw them, known and understood in the Department. Sometimes a minister would chair the Chairmen's meeting; sometimes it would fall to Archie Rennie or to me. The senior Department officer most closely concerned chaired each of the others. Drafts of departmental circulars were circulated, and discussed and occasionally mangled at one or more of these gatherings before issue.

To the Chairmen we offered a modest lunch sent down from the canteen; the others usually began their meetings later and had to be content with tea and biscuits. We all knew each other pretty well; and if the Secretary of State, his officers, members of the boards and their officers might be regarded in some ways as an extended family, it would be untrue to suggest that, any more than members of other families, we always saw eye to eye. Ultimately, however, we all had to work together, and we managed to do so quite effectively.

Every two years the four-year appointments of half the members of each board came to an end; and making new appointments or re-appointments was a major exercise. Membership of boards had to reflect many interests. There had to be some doctors and members of other professions, members of local authorities, trades unions and voluntary bodies. We sought nominations from a great number of statutory and other bodies; not every interest could be represented all the time. In fact, members were not representative in the strict sense at all; they were people of different backgrounds appointed by the Secretary of State to act in a personal capacity as board members. It usually fell to me to consult chairmen individually about the nominations received, about the possible future make-up of the board, and about a possible successor in the chair if he or she were retiring. Then with my colleagues I had to put together a submission to ministers, one for each board, making recommendations for future membership. What followed varied. The recommendations might be accepted; there might be requests for more information; there might be exchanges of notes or talks as a result of which names might be dropped or new names brought forward. We were always glad when at last we had fifteen lists of names agreed by the Secretary of State. In these days, political considerations were never a significant issue — indeed George Younger excited consternation among some of his political supporters by appointing a former Labour parliamentary candidate as chairman of one of the major boards.

It was for the boards to run the service locally, to employ the staff, to establish new units, to maintain the buildings and generally to improve the facilities available to the local people. But the Secretary of State by his overall control determined the pace of development of the service and the direction in which it was going. Finance was a crucial limiting factor. Nearly all the money available to boards came from the Secretary of State. Once the total annual sums to be available for health services in Scotland had been determined in the higher corridors of power in Whitehall and St. Andrew's House, we in the Department made an allocation to each board on the basis of a complicated, but generally accepted, formula known as SHARE. This took account not only of boards' existing commitments, but the need to provide relatively more money for those boards whose facilities, for historical reasons, were less extensive than those in other areas. But formula or no formula, there was still room for argument by those — and that was sometimes everyone — who thought they were not getting enough to cover inflation, advances in medicine, pay increases or particular local difficulties. How many hours did I spend with successive ministers before, during and after their meetings with chairmen or with hard-pressed boards who wondered how they could stay out of the red? Somehow, costs were cut or temporary cover was found. Nonetheless, as year succeeded year expenditure in real terms increased. So of course, did people's expectations.

Boards in Scotland may have thought they were underfunded, but NHS expenditure in Scotland per head of population was about 25% higher than in England and Wales. There were some compelling reasons for higher expenditure in Scotland. Teaching hospitals formed a larger proportion of the hospital service, and they cost much more to run than non-teaching hospitals. It is more expensive to provide services in areas of sparse and scattered population, and there are more off-shore islands, and more moorland and mountain in Scotland than south of the border. But these factors could not account for the whole of the 25% difference which had emerged over the years. Scottish ministers could not publicise this advantage as much as they would have wished. Too much said about it might encourage plots in Whitehall or Westminster to divert some of this extra money elsewhere.

Health services will probably always be plagued by financial problems. The advance of medical knowledge and techniques goes on relentlessly. It becomes possible to treat, often at considerable expense, patients who could not have been treated before. As more people survive acute illness, they live longer and become candidates for long-term geriatric care. The demands for health care could indeed be infinite, for there is always room for some improvement in bodily function even among those not actually ill. There are always demands, too, for more to be spent on prevention (is prevention not better than cure?) even though it may be difficult to identify the return from the money spent. In a nationally funded health service governments have to set limits to expenditure that in a private system of medical care, even where insurance-funded, are set by the market. Much of my time was, as a result, spent thinking about, writing about and arguing about money.

Whatever the funds available, there is always room for debate about what they should be spent on. Services already on the ground have to be paid for in the short term at least; but as medicine advances, and as the age structure of the population changes, future needs will not be the same as present needs. How far can they be predicted, planned for and provision made at the right time? Is it indeed always a question of 'needs' — a word which suggests something objective beyond debate? Is it not rather a matter of priorities or even simple (or not so simple) choices? It was part of the job of our Departmental Planning Unit to brood upon such difficult matters. Its head, Dr John Grant, and I would from time to time sit in my room looking out over the Old Town of Edinburgh trying to peer into the future. The Scottish Health Services Planning Council had a working party on Health Priorities of which we were both members and for which we prepared most of the material. Its Chairman was Mr John Wallace, actuary, former member of a health board, retired general manager of a major insurance company, and still an active mountaineer.

The Working Party produced in 1980 a report entitled 'Scottish Health Priorities for the Eighties', its acronym SHAPE being as appropriate to its concerns as was SHARE in another field. Apart from urging that more effort be devoted to the prevention of illness, its main conclusion was that more priority had to be given to geriatric and long stay services. This was not perhaps surprising, granted what everyone knew about the increasing numbers of elderly in the community. But these were views not normally given much support in the high-powered units of the acute hospitals operating at the frontiers of medicine, and it was valuable to have the Working Party's conclusions supported by extensive data and argument. The Secretary of State urged health boards to make the report the basis of their planning of local services.

The range of subjects which came my way lent variety, and spice, to my official life. We received proposals for building new hospitals and for closing old ones. Even the dreariest establishment, criticised for years by local people, suddenly found vocal defenders when a board proposed to close it. We were concerned about waiting times for admission to some departments of general hospitals, and pressed for local action to reduce it. The fact that some people had to wait so long for hospital care always seemed to me one of the most unsatisfactory features of the NHS. It was all too easy to argue that more resources were needed — some people's solution for almost every problem. Though some progress was made I was never convinced that more could not have been done within existing resources by intensive efforts on the ground, if not to solve the problem, at least to reduce waiting times and waiting lists dramatically.

Some patients are too easily forgotten — those suffering from mental handicap, for example. Many of these were housed in old Victorian buildings — which offered much needed 'asylum' in their day — or other less than satisfactory accommodation. We had a long-running and not altogether successful campaign with one of the boards to bring these patients up their list of priorities. The claims of modern technology on the other hand are seldom forgotten. With the help of a committee of the Planning Council and health board representatives we reached agreement on a plan for the purchase, use and distribution of major computers.

There was seldom a day in which my official thoughts did not turn at some time to sex in one or other of its manifestations, implications or complications. Contraception, abortion, in vitro fertilisation and other headline-grabbing subjects were dealt with by one of my divisions. The assistant secretary, Ted Redmond, and his successor Betty Craghill had to spend even more time on them than I. One late afternoon Betty Craghill, a resilient character, but sorely tried that day, put her head round my door and said, 'I've had enough for one day — surrogate mothers, artificial insemination, teenage pregnancies . . . the lot. I'm going home.'

If abortion was not always with us it was seldom far away. Successive governments had taken the view that legislation on this subject was for Private Members, not the government, to initiate; and there always seemed to be some Private Member with proposals in his pocket or a Bill before the House to amend the 1967 Act (itself introduced by a Private Member, Mr David Steel, alias the Boy David, thought by some to have been taken for a ride by pro-abortion zealots). Even although the running was made by Private Members, the health ministers and their departments were expected to have views on the implications of the latest proposals or even to offer help with drafting. Although these proposals regularly ran into the sands of controversy or were defeated in the House, the tally of official time spent over the years on the subject in the office or official box was considerable.

Contraception is not normally a matter into which Secretaries of State have to pronounce, but the kind of publicity to be put out on the subject by health service bodies was certainly a matter into which ministers were willy-nilly drawn. I and my colleagues had from time to time to sit and contemplate some eye-catching publicity which the Scottish Health Education Group proposed to issue and ask ourselves whether the Secretary of State would be prepared to defend its appearance in the public prints. However much they might want to give SHEG, as it was known, a free rein in the publicity field, ministers supplied its funds and therefore could not completely disclaim responsibility for what it did. Sometimes we felt confident enough to give the all-clear ourselves; but on other occasions we declined to be heroic and submitted the doubtful material to ministers. They, after all, would have to answer for it, not us.

It was in the nature of SHEG's activities that they should arouse controversy from time to time. Even if some of their effort had to be devoted to humdrum campaigns about cleaning teeth or taking exercise, their publicity had to be lively and even provocative, if it was to make an impact. More of their effort was directed to informing the public of the dangers of smoking and of over-indulgence in alcohol. Here too we were involved in controversy, but the controversy related not so much to SHEG's publicity as to the substance of Government policies.

Files on tobacco and alcohol often landed on my desk, and on these issues we worked closely with DHSS. Medical and statistical evidence indicated that all cigarette smoking and over-indulgence in alcohol was dangerous to health. Successive governments had accepted this evidence, and although some of it was not completely free from challenge, the main controversies related to what the government of the day did or failed to do about it. Different policies of varying severity were urged upon ministers by various pressure groups — tobacco advertising should be banned; advertising should be strictly controlled in relation to both tobacco and alcohol; smoking should be banned in public places; tobacco and alcohol should be taxed much more heavily. Everyone knew that powerful vested interests were involved; the financial implications for the producers and for the Government were enormous; and many people's jobs could be affected. I came nearer than at any time in my career to a row with a colleague — in another Scottish department — when it was in effect argued that the question of jobs of tobacco workers in the west of Scotland took priority over the fact that their activities helped to condemn some of their neighbours to an early grave.

I sometimes joined colleagues from DHSS at meetings with the Tobacco Advisory Council, which in spite of its high sounding name, was merely the trade organisation for the tobacco industry. Gradually, as the result of pressure on the companies, the screw was turned tighter on cigarette advertising, and public opinion came to accept more and more restrictions on smoking in public places. But these developments came by agreement, persuasion and arm-twisting, not always by the Government, and we continued to be at the receiving end of representations from those who continued to be disappointed that the Government did not make a more resolute attack on dangerous practices known to need a 'health warning'.

Even in what might be expected to be less controversial fields, the Department was often at the centre of debate. Advisory groups, official and otherwise, produced report after report on some aspect of health care. Sometimes their conclusions were disputed, but there were always those who thought that their recommendations should be given top priority. The Department had to advise the Secretary of State on the action he should take, especially on reports which came from the Planning Council. When a specially appointed and highly qualified group recommended that for a variety of well argued reasons open-heart surgery should be restricted to highly-specialised units in Edinburgh and Glasgow, people in Aberdeen were not at all happy. The Secretary of State decided nonetheless to accept its conclusions. A campaign rumbled on for years . . . and in due course provision for open-heart surgery was made in Aberdeen.

The mental health field could produce high drama as well as its share of controversy. On 30th November 1976 when I was still in SED, two patients had managed to escape from the State Hospital at Carstairs, a secure institution occupied by dangerous, violent or criminal patients. In the course of their escape they killed three people — a member of the staff, another patient and a policeman. Dreadful enough in itself, this incident was followed by the passing of a resolution by about three hundred staff, to the effect that senior members of the medical and nursing staff be suspended. This was followed by the threat of a strike and exclusion of senior staff from the hospital. The Secretary of State announced that a public enquiry would be held, and after a few shattering days in which there were discussions involving Harry Ewing, the junior minister, and leaders of the union, staffing arrangements at the hospital were restored to something like normality.

Because of its special nature the hospital was managed not by the Lanarkshire Health Board in whose area it was situated, but by a separate Management Committee of which the chairman was the assistant secretary in the Department who dealt with mental health. The Department therefore had a closer relationship with the State Hospital than with any other individual hospital in Scotland. The shock of these events was still very much in the minds of George Robertson, the assistant secretary now concerned, and his colleagues when I first discussed the situation with him after my arrival in Room 117. A *modus vivendi* had been established at the hospital, but everyone was waiting for the report of the public enquiry being conducted by Sheriff Principal R. Reid QC. That report was published early in October 1977, and we immediately had to consider its recommendations for the future management and running of the hospital. It was George who had the main burden of drafting a submission to the Secretary of State about the action to be taken. I and then Archie Rennie went over this with considerable care. As a result of the Secretary of State's decisions on the final version presented to him we had a complete plan for the changes to be made on various fronts, including, in particular, arrangements for security. It was now for the Management Committee (which like health boards included people of various backgrounds) to put the new arrangements into operation. They could not all be implemented overnight — there was for example a good deal of building work to be done — and my periodic discussions with George about progress being made went on for some months.

There was another dramatic incident when a patient at a mental hospital managed to leave the hospital and go to the grounds of another hospital where he murdered his wife, daughter and brother-in-law. He had been in the care of the first hospital by order of the Sheriff, but without formal restriction, following an earlier attempted murder. Once again this was terrible enough in itself, and there was inevitably some embarrassment for the Secretary of State. It raised many questions about the referral of patients by the court to mental hospitals and the arrangements for their custody. We had to follow up these questions with the authorities concerned and with ministers — again a process lasting several months.

Since some patients in mental hospitals are subject to legal restraints of various kinds, the administration of these hospitals is governed by statute to a much greater degree than other hospitals. While most members of the staff of my divisions had only occasional need to refer to the National Health Service (Scotland) Acts, those concerned with mental hospitals had to have the relevant

Acts and Regulations ever at hand on their desks. In the light of experience of the working of existing statutory procedures, and in the light too of growing pressures to keep restrictions on patients to the minimum consistent with the safety of the public, it became apparent in the later seventies that the existing mental health legislation ought to be reviewed. We carried out just such a review and prepared proposals for changes in the statutes. The consultation with interested bodies and with ministers, the securing of a place in the Parliamentary timetable, the consideration of drafts prepared by the parliamentary draftsman — all this takes a great deal of time, even if, as in this case, it was not what Parliament and public might regard as major legislation. Once a certain stage was reached, some staff already experienced on mental health had to be withdrawn from other work and employed full-time on the Bill.

In the work on a Bill of this kind, an under secretary with many other subjects to cover cannot be an expert on the detail; he can only have a general supervisory role, concerned with the major issues and the general progress of the work. Such was my limited function. Once our Bill was before Parliament (it started in the Lords) it was for the assistant secretary, by now Angus Macpherson, his principal Bill Giles, and legal and medical colleagues to carry the main burden of briefing ministers and being available in the Official Box. At one stage it seemed as if all our efforts might come to nothing. Not long after the Bill reached the Commons in the spring of 1983 a general election was announced. It did not look as if it could complete its passage before Parliament was dissolved. But the Bill was not politically controversial, and by cooperation between Government and Opposition the timetable for considering it in the House was drastically revised and its passage secured — just.

In spite of the large sums being spent on the health service in Scotland the health record of the people of Scotland was, and remains, in some respects abysmal. The only European country with high rates of heart disease and lung cancer comparable to ours is Finland; and in both countries alcoholism is a major social and medical problem. Discussions between the Chief Medical Officers of the two countries resulted in a formal agreement for the joint study of these and other common problems. With three professional colleagues I went to Finland to learn more about how their health service worked, and to make detailed arrangements for following up this agreement. We had an intensive few days of meetings and visits. We found that no official visit to Finland was complete without a sauna appearing on the programme. The sauna has an important, almost mystical, place in Finnish life and lore — so important that I did not confess to our friendly and hospitable hosts that its attractions were lost on me.

A few years later, as part of a review of progress with our joint studies, the Finns invited our Chief Medical Officer, Dr John Reid, and myself — and our wives — to visit Lapland. Such problems as we have in Scotland in providing health services in what we call remote areas do not compare with the difficulties of the much more remote and scattered communities of northern Lapland far beyond the Arctic Circle. On our first day at lunch in the most northerly health centre in Finland, our hosts, eager to give us the real flavour of the country, provided reindeer meat for the main course and cloudberries for the dessert. On the next day, further south, the staff of another health centre were determined that we should enjoy typical local fare — and we had reindeer and cloudberries. On the third day . . . no; the men from Helsinki who were with us had passed on the message.

We brought back with us lively impressions not only of remote health centres, resilient staff and patients, but also of long, long roads, endless forests, road signs urging us to beware of elks, an open air museum consisting of a variety of ingenious devices for trapping bears — and of course the inevitable sauna, or rather saunas; one male, one female.

Whether on these exceptional forays into foreign parts or on everyday work at home I worked closely as in the past with professional colleagues — doctors, nurses, lawyers, especially the doctors. With one other group I had rather more dealings than in the past — the staff, mostly journalists, of the Press Office, or rather the Scottish Information Office to give it its correct name. They issued Press Notices about new developments, newly-published reports and ministers' speeches; they were at the receiving end of queries from what was by then called the 'media', queries which had to be given replies as soon as possible. On the detailed points concerning my side of the Department a press officer would go to the assistant secretary or principal; on more general or more sensitive issues they would come to me. Press officers do not come from any Civil Service mould; our exchanges were often lively and sometimes entertaining.

In our daily perusal of the papers we regularly came across stories which presented a curious selection of the facts as we knew them. Only occasionally when the departure from reality was grossly misleading or unfair did we decide that some kind of correction or protest was needed. Not that it always did much good. I was more often amused than dismayed by the apparent eagerness of some of those employed in the media to reject the straightforward explanation of a situation when it was possible to think up a sinister one. Sometimes it is the little things which irritate. Even acknowledging the convenience of short words, particularly in headlines, I found it very tiresome when the word 'row' was used, as it so often was, to describe anything from a routine, amicable difference of view to an acrimonious dispute.

From time to time during the latter part of the seventies all of us in St. Andrew's House had to look beyond our immediate concerns and consider how the services for which we were responsible would be affected by Government proposals for Scottish devolution. I had had my share of this in SED, and when I transferred to health was caught up in considering the health implications of proposals which were soon enshrined in the Scotland Bill, introduced in November 1977. The Bill proposed the setting up of a Scottish Assembly. Most Government responsibilities for health would be removed from Westminster and the Secretary of State for Scotland, and transferred to a Scottish Assembly in which there would be a minister responsible for health. I had no personal enthusiasm for what was proposed, being by no means convinced that it would do very much for the general well-being of Scotland. But that was not a view which I trumpeted abroad. The formation of proposals for running the health service within the Government's chosen scheme of devolution was just another job to be done diligently as a Government servant. In due course what became the Scotland Act contained a requirement that the scheme of devolution should be implemented only after a referendum to test public acceptance. I was not sorry when it became apparent that there were sufficient sceptics like myself among the Scottish people. The required percentage of votes in favour was not achieved. The whole scheme, on which seemingly endless words had been written and spoken, lapsed. I never saw another file marked 'Devolution' for the rest of my career.

In many respects the mechanics of administration in St. Andrew's House in the early 1980s were not much different from what they had been when I saw my first file in 1947. Modern management techniques for dealing with large blocks of routine work — handling orders for supplies; considering applications for social security allowances — were hardly relevant to the work of a ministerial headquarters office. Ministerial correspondence had still to be dealt with, draft replies to PQs prepared, meetings held, minutes written, circulars drafted — all in the time honoured way.

Or not quite; advances in technology had not passed us by. Copies of documents could now be produced in a few seconds; electronic typewriters were everywhere, and the first word processors could be seen in certain favoured locations; facsimiles of papers received in London could appear within minutes on desks in Edinburgh. It was now possible for officials sitting round a 'remote table' in Edinburgh to have meetings with ministers sitting at a similar table in Dover House. Each of these tables, connected by direct line, had a loudspeaker and a number of individual microphones, opposite which sat the participants. Apart from the absence of visual reactions, discussion could go on almost as easily as it could at a single table. No doubt one of these days, there will be visual contact as well.

Time had marched on in other ways. My senior colleagues of the 1940s would have been surprised and perhaps shocked to see young women in slacks and young men in shirt sleeves without jackets. Winter brought out more anoraks than overcoats. In the petrol-rationed post-war days only a few spaces in the car park had been occupied; now, too many cars chased too few spaces, and there was an elaborate scheme for allocating those available. In the canteen waitresses were no more; self service, and, for many, fast food, were the order of the day.

There had been some changes in the structure of the civil service, none very dramatic; and the only one which affected me personally had no practical significance. A system of grading by numbers had been introduced covering both professionals and administrators. Under secretaries and their professional equivalents were now formally known as 'Grade 3'. In spite of this the Deputy Chief Medical Officer was still the Deputy Chief Medical Officer, under secretaries were still called under secretaries, and there was no doubt at all that the Secretary (formally Grade 2) was still the Secretary.

Nor had the basic machinery of government changed in any significant way. We were still responsible to ministers and they were responsible to Parliament. This meant for me and my senior colleagues, as it had for our predecessors down the years, frequent walks along the corridor to the ministers' rooms and visits to Westminster, frequent or occasional, depending on business at the time.

There was one annual Parliamentary occasion for which I regularly led a small team to Westminster. This was what was known, rather misleadingly, as the Estimates Debate. It was in fact a morning debate in the Scottish Grand Committee about the general running of the NHS on a procedural motion about the funds being made available. Any aspect of the service, general or particular, could be raised without advance notice — the condition of the buildings at a cottage hospital in a Members' constituency; the adequacy of the total sum provided for running the service in Scotland; the need for more staff here, or better food there; the failure of a health board to give sufficient priority to patients suffering from any one of the many ills which can afflict us.

It was not difficult to draft an opening speech for the minister giving some account of current progress, emphasising the good news but acknowledging the problems. He might amend it here and there or dress it up with some political comment — that was up to him. We could not, however, anticipate everything which might be raised in the debate. All we could do was draw up a list of the major current concerns, prepare notes on each one, go over them with the minister if he wished, write more notes on other topics he wanted covered, take with us to the debate key papers and a fat file of statistics — and hope for the best. After all, the minister would not have time to reply to everything in his closing speech. He could reply to those points on which he had answers, and undertake to look into the others.

In the committee room, as in the House itself, Members sit on rows of benches facing each other from which they can glare or jeer at their opponents or even listen to what they have to say. But unlike the House there is a kind of top table at right angles to, and a foot or so higher than, Members' benches. In the middle of this table sits the chairman; on his left are officials of the House and on his right sit officials from the minister's department. Ministers themselves sit at the end of the front bench on the chairman's right and a few feet away from the officials from the department. By a unusual inversion of the natural order of things, the officials look down on the minister; and the minister has to stand up to speak to them.

As these debates went on, I or one of my colleagues would write a sentence or two if we could on points raised which were not already covered in the notes; and these additional notes would be handed down to the minister. If he were too engrossed and we could not attract his attention, sign language would persuade one of his colleagues behind him to tap him on the shoulder or even poke him in the ribs. From time to time the minister would come over for a brief *sotto voce* discussion. Occasionally if a Member raised some startling point new to us on which the minister ought if possible to say something, I would ask one of my colleagues to move smartly to the nearest telephone and speak to someone in St. Andrew's House or, if need be, a health board.

There was only one occasion in the course of these several debates when I remember being slightly taken aback. The chairman on that day was Harry Gourlay, Labour MP for one of the Fife constituencies. I had sat at his right elbow all morning and he had said nothing, not even 'Good Morning'. Suddenly when Tam Dalyell was on his feet airing one of his well-known obsessions, a voice spoke in my left ear: 'Typical Etonian arrogance.' Having thus delivered to an anonymous official an indication of the respect he had for his party comrade, Mr Gourlay lapsed into silence and never spoke again.

For a few years there had been at the back of my mind an awareness that I would retire on 16th June 1983. Unlike a few of my colleagues I never kept a count of the number of working days to go. It seemed in the last couple of years before D-day that time flew by even more quickly than it used to. I had on the whole enjoyed my work, but I would not be devastated when I no longer had to go to the office every morning. As winter turned to spring in 1983, there were more and more occasions when I realised I would not be there to deal with the next chapter of an unfolding story. Was the flow of paper not becoming less than might have been expected? Were my colleagues perhaps saying to themselves that there was little point in involving me in some particular exercise? Whether they were or not, we all experienced a marked drop in the volume of paper when a general election was announced. Senior civil servants in such circumstances normally busy themselves with the preparation of notes for incoming ministers — perhaps two sets, if betting on the outcome of the election is difficult and there is high political content in the work of the department.

Allowing for leave to which I was entitled, I had arranged that my last day would be, as it later turned out, the day before polling day. I took only a limited interest in the preparation of notes for ministers I would never see. With more time on my hands than I had for years I found my times of arrival at and departure from the office coming closer together. In between I devoted more attention than usual to the pages of the *Lancet* and *British Medical Journal*. There were reports about a medical phenomenon causing increasing interest and concern in America. Patients were dying because the bodily mechanisms which normally resisted the onset of ordinary infections were not working. All these patients were male homosexuals. Would this phenomenon cross the Atlantic? If it did, and we were faced with a new public health problem, I would be away before any files came to Room 117.

I had attended down the years many presentations to colleagues about to retire. At one of the first, the senior officer who was the recipient of our good wishes had become quite emotional when he said that in a few moments he would walk down the stairs of St. Andrew's House for the last time. On a few occasions there were some mildly embarrassing moments, but displays of emotion were not typical of these gatherings. Normally after a senior official had spoken and made the presentation, the recipient thanked the assembled company for their good wishes and for whatever he might have chosen as the tangible expression of their esteem (on one occasion when I made the presentation it was a chain-saw!) with some perhaps awkward, perhaps amusing, recollections of life in the bureaucracy.

When my own turn came on the afternoon of 8th June my wife was present with me. Archie Rennie included in the generous remarks expected on such occasions a reference to my being one of the more detached members of the Department. Fair comment; I was never an 'organisation man' and no doubt it showed from time to time. I responded in what I hope were suitable terms. We all did justice to the splendid tea organised by Iris Paterson and other female colleagues; there were handshakes, recollections of experiences shared in days gone by, badinage and good wishes. I walked down the stairs and remembered my senior colleague of many years before only when I was outside the door.

Next morning at 9.00 a.m., after the first rush of early activity at the polling stations, when my former colleagues were settling down at their desks, my wife and I were on an aircraft *en route* to the south of France.